I0760179

The JACK VAN LOAN Story

Others have described Jack as tough or strong, but I'd add to that a sense of clear-eyed determination. Jack felt it important that we were fully aware of the treatment of our POWs at the hands of the Hanoi regime. He tells us firsthand, how our captive pilots were treated. This is an important chapter in our history because it provides a clear distinction about the America that Jack loved so much. It would be hard to find examples of American mistreatment of POWs.

Jack's fellow prisoners credit him with holding them together and helping them survive. He certainly did that and well deserves the title of "American Patriot."

—*Ron Hagell*, President, Chapter 303, Vietnam Veterans of America

"If you're going to be in a prison camp, choose this guy as a cell mate. He's a LIFESAVER!"

—*Charlie Plumb*, fellow long term Hanoi Hilton POW

Jack was my first cellmate in Hanoi. I had been badly injured during ejection, and Jack was integral in my healing. Jack literally saved my life! Jack was a man of superior intellect, great compassion, and impeccable honor and integrity. It was my absolute honor and privilege to call Jack my friend.

—*Read Mecleary*, fellow long-term Hanoi Hilton POW

The Jack Van Loan Story

In His Own Words

Foreword by Norman Turner

Final Comments by Glenn Van Loan

Red Engine Press
Fort Smith, Arkansas

EDITED BY BOB DOERR

COVER DESIGN BY JOYCE FAULKNER

BACK COVER PHOTO COURTESY OF RON HAGELL

LIBRARY OF CONGRESS CONTROL NUMBER: 2023950611

ISBN: 979-8-9879576-9-1 (softcover)

ISBN: 979-8-9895620-0-8 (hardcover)

Jack Van Loan
1954

Table of Contents

FOREWORD

Wars and combat have historically brought out the best and the worst in human behavior. Such was the case of the American prisoners of war, some of whom were held for many years under atrocious conditions in North Vietnam. The ratio of conduct with this group is very heavily loaded toward the best, with so many men demonstrating incredible standards of patriotism, honor and extraordinary heroism.

Being a prisoner is not in itself heroic. This situation usually starts as an unfortunate turn of events and, in the beginning, makes the subject merely an unfortunate victim of the vagaries of fortune. However, the manner in which a man responds and adjusts to the tremendous pressures and tribulations of the state in which he finds himself reveals his true character.

Those held in North Vietnam exhibited the entire range of possible conduct, from gallantry and heroism above and beyond the call of duty to acts of shameful cowardice. Men such as Jim Stockdale, who was awarded the Medal of Honor, and others including Robbie Risner, Jerimiah Denton, and Larry Guarino who probably should have been, were heroic beyond belief or understanding. They suffered unbearable tortures yet never broke faith with their fellow warriors.

The motto of the 4th Allied POW Wing, comprised of the POWs in North Vietnam, is "Return with Honor." That is what they wanted to do, and for the most part, they did exactly that. One of the best of the best was then Major Jack Van Loan who was shot down over North Vietnam flying an F-4 Phantom II fighter on the 20th of May 1967. He spent almost six years in confinement under often terrifying and painful conditions as prisoner of a brutal regime. He never failed to maintain loyalty to and support for his brothers at war. In my opinion, several of them owe their lives to him.

This is his story and that of the men with whom he shared his experiences. They continued to fight from their cells by resisting the attempts by North Vietnamese captors to coerce them to denounce America or ask for special treatment. Almost without exception, they stood by their comrades, helping each other and resisting to the best of their ability. As Jack and others have stated, "All gave some and some gave all." The fear, pain, and loneliness suffered by these men, and how they responded to those trials, comprises a shining tribute to the quality of character of the great majority of our warriors.

I was a fighter pilot in Southeast Asia also, flying the same type aircraft on my second tour as did Jack. We were all aware of the possibility of becoming POWs if we were shot down. I was never afraid of being killed, but I did have a great dread of being captured and couldn't think of anything more frightening. Needless to say, my respect for Jack and others of this group is beyond my ability to express adequately. I am proud that he is my friend.

—***Norman Turner***, Lt. Col. (Ret), USAF

Editor's Comments

This past year when the family and a friend of Jack Van Loan reached out to me for assistance in getting the very rough draft of Jack's memoir published, I felt an instant obligation to help them. I had many personal reasons.

Like Jack, I was a career USAF officer and even served a tour of duty in Thailand. I had a further bond in that my father was a pilot and a POW in Germany during WWII. At the time I received the request, I was the president of the Military Writers Society of America. Helping his family get the book published fit into two of MWSA's founding principles: (1) preserve history one story at a time, and (2) encourage writing as a form of therapy for veterans and their families.

Reading Jack's manuscript, it is easy to see why he needed to tell his story. While Jack passed away a number of years ago, the story still deserved to see the light of day. Not just for Jack's family, but for anyone who has an interest in learning about the POW experience so many of our American military members went through in North Vietnam.

That experience is admittedly difficult to read about and more difficult to fully grasp. Jack's description of it is not sugar coated. As bad as it was for him, he readily admits that others had it worse. I can't imagine the torture Jack and his fellow prisoners went through. Nor can I fully appreciate being kept a prisoner for six years in the conditions they had to endure.

This final product was compiled from Jack's draft memoir. Most of it was documented long after his release and return to the U.S. He readily states in the manuscript that it was difficult to keep track of dates while he was in "jail."

Although I have not been able to confirm that all of the names of individuals he mentions as being fellow POWs were correct, I have no doubt they were there. Jack either forgot the actual name a decade or two after his return, or he misnamed the individual on purpose.

This is Jack's story in his words. It is not a biography. While I did a lot of reorganizing and editing, I did my best not to change what he wrote or his "voice" that comes through quite clear.

One of the hardest things I had to fight against was turning Jack's memoir into a much longer book with a lot more detail regarding the broader POW experience. Other POWs have written books or have had books written about them. Various government entities have produced studies or papers on the topic.

My original goal in doing this extra research focused on gathering additional data on Jack. However, it seemed to me like all the books or articles I found had other stories that wanted to suck me in deeper. Despite my growing fascination with this broader research, I knew my task was to get Jack's story published and not rewrite one of my own.

However, I did uncover a few comments about Jack that were worth noting. In what may be the premier account of the POW experience in southeast Asia, 1961-73, *Honor Bound*, by Stuart I. Rochester and Frederick Kiley, I found the following passages about Jack:

> Lt. Cmdr. Richard Stratton a fellow POW, who was placed in solitary confinement without any light for seven weeks, credits his remaining sane to Jack's tapping on the adjacent wall with news and time hacks (pp 349).
>
> Maj. Bud Day included Jack as one of the toughest, gutsy people in the Plantation POW camp (pp 378). The book also cited Jack's story telling ability, specifically mentioning "Gone with the Wind," (pp 423).
>
> Separately, in his book Surviving Hell: A POWs Journey, fellow POW Maj. Leo Thorsness did the same, calling Jack one of the great "story reporters," referring to his rendition of "Gone with the Wind."

All the reference material I found had reports of the rope torture, the ankle shackles, the frequent beatings, and other atrocities most of us can hardly imagine. I also found substantial corroboration that the most brutal torture stopped after Ho's death. As a result, the accounts of treatment by the North Vietnamese by those captured after Ho's death reflect an experience much different than what Jack and the others experienced.

I appreciate having the opportunity to assist in getting this book published. It is a story all military historians need to read, and one that anyone who is interested in the Vietnam conflict should.

—***Bob Doerr***

Chapter 1 ★ Darkness Falls

WE WERE HIT A MORTAL BLOW from the MiG. When the control stick in my cockpit froze up completely, rigid as though it was welded in place, I shouted, "Get out!" to my back seater. I then waited about two nanoseconds before pulling the ejection handle between my legs. There was an instantaneous deafening boom and I felt the violent punch as the seat fired. I was out and into the whipping wind. As I saw myself clear the airplane in the seat, I heard a terrific explosion, and the airplane vaporized right underneath me.

A few moments later, the seat separated from me with a jarring tug. I looked up and saw that I was under the canopy of the deployed parachute. Glancing down, the biggest pieces of the airplane I could see appeared to be about the size of your hat.

The 45,000-pound fighter, my F-4 Phantom II, that had been my chariot and barrier against the world and elements just a few seconds before had blown to a thousand pieces right underneath me. I couldn't believe it. I still don't understand how the fragments didn't hit me.

If I hadn't decided years before what I would do if the control stick ever froze and had made up my mind that I would get out immediately, it would all have been over right then. If I had just sat there and hit the paddle switch or reached for a circuit breaker or something like that, both of us would have died right on the spot, blown away forever. But I grabbed the ejection handle without hesitation, and both of us were alive and out into the open sky.

Once I stabilized in my parachute, I looked around and immediately spotted Joe Milligan, my back seater. He had ejected safely and had a good chute. We were so close together that we could have almost shaken hands coming down. As we descended toward the green growth below us, I was surprised to see the MiGs turning in toward us. With a sense of dismay that soon turned to anger, I saw and heard the cannons on the fighters as they started to strafe us. I looked right at them as they tried to murder us in our parachutes.

It was a stupid move, I suppose, but I got my .38 loose and fired at them as they went by. I gave them all six shots. It was like that cartoon you have seen, the last great act of defiance, where an eagle is diving down and about to devour a mouse, and the mouse is standing there, just giving him the finger. That was about how effective it was. It was my last great act of defiance for a good while.

Then, almost immediately, I saw some F-4s come roaring by. Years later, I confirmed that the rest of my flight—Robin Olds, Bob Pardo, and Ron Catton—had returned and chased the MiGs away. Things became quieter as I floated down in my parachute over the brilliant green landscape. Soon after that, the ground came up to meet me, and I slammed down onto Thud Ridge.

When we got into the fight with the MiGs, my UHF radio was constantly channelizing. The radio in the F-4 made a particular noise when you changed from one channel to another. This told you that an action was in process. When it stopped, you were on the new channel and could communicate. Once in a while, a radio would malfunction and start channelizing through the frequencies on its own. Sometimes this was a temporary condition, and if you waited, the radio would start working again. On other occasions, the channelizing did not stop, and that meant that during this period you were deaf and mute to oral communications to and from your ship.

Years later, Bob Pardo told me that just before I was shot down, "We were all hollering at you to break right, break right." Of course, I never heard a damn thing through the radio. That was a bit of a tough break and the result of bad judgment on my part. I will explain later, but you pay your dollar and take your chances.

Upon landing, I smashed my knee against a tree and seriously damaged it. It hurt like hell. My plastic and metal clipboard that had been on my knee was blown away by the wind blast shortly after I ejected, and it had hit me in the face. I had two or three pretty deep lacerations on my chin from it.

Joe had landed close by, and after freeing ourselves from the parachutes, we got together. His face was red and singed where he had been burned by the explosion of the airplane. Still, we were alive and damn lucky to be that way, all things considered. A profusion of thoughts and emotions ran through my mind. Fear and dread were the prevalent sensations at that point, but there was also a current of adrenalin rush and the constant pain from my injuries.

There we stood, alone and lost in a strange land. We were in a state of shock standing there at the top of Thud Ridge. I told Joe to hide, but to this day I wish we had tried to go down the ridge immediately and headed east as far as we possibly could. Only then should we have tried to hide.

I've looked back with regret on that critical moment many times. All of our survival training had taught us that you hide during hours of daylight and move at night. It was about four o'clock in the afternoon, and at the time, I thought that we would just hide there for a while. If possible, we would head for the coast after it got dark.

Unfortunately, as I realized later, my reasoning was flawed. We did hide, but the bad guys had us triangulated as we came down in our chutes. Soon, there were people running around everywhere looking for us. Christ, that place was just overrun with Vietnamese! Pretty soon we heard the noise of people moving close in all around us. We stayed as quiet as possible, barely breathing. It was terrifying.

Then, with anticlimactic understatement, a young boy appeared and stood there looking at us. He'd found us hiding under a bush and pointed an antique French musket at us. The end of that monster looked as big around as a cannon. The kid was about twelve years old. He held this massive collector's item that looked as though it might have been used against Wellington at Waterloo. He waved it around, the muzzle moving in circles in our general direction.

Keeping as immobile as I could, I mumbled to Joe, "Keep your hands up and don't move around. If that kid pulls the trigger, three people are going to die, him and both of us. That damn thing will blow up."

Pretty soon the rest of the ragtag militia came up, pointing AK-47s at us. We knew then that the whole deal was over. We were captured. They stripped us of our flight suits and gear. They found our parachutes, and then through sign language, they gestured for us to move down the mountain. So, I started the long walk down the slope, limping badly because of the pain from my seriously damaged knee.

I thought about my situation, deciding that this was the end of that war and the beginning of another one. Boy was I right. I'll tell you this, I knew a hell of a lot more about that war than the Vietnamese did. And I knew a hell of a lot more about Ho Chi Minh than they did. I realized that right away, and that surprised them. It also pissed them off.

As I mentioned, my left knee slammed up against the tree pretty hard when I landed in the chute. It was badly twisted, and I could see it swelling up right in front of me. It got pretty big, and I had difficulty walking. I had blood all over me from various cuts and lacerations, but those wounds weren't debilitating like my knee injury was. I started down off Thud Ridge in my underwear, with the end of an AK-47 poked in my back. My hands were tied behind my back too. My new war was just beginning, and what a hell of a war it would be.

In the end, we lost 56,000 Americans, and we had hundreds of thousands wounded. Billions in the national treasure were lost. However, the biggest loss of all...out of the whole Vietnam War...was the loss of confidence in our government. An impression that still exists today. A man's perspective of war is entirely different when he's been shot at and hit.

Chapter 2★ The Welcome

MY CAPTORS TOOK ME TO SEVEN flack sites. Interspersed among them were three different army camps. I was paraded around with the guards insisting that my head be down and my hands be up once they were untied. They were displaying the Yankee air pirate for the folks, and it occurred to me that these people weren't all that keen on keeping with the Geneva convention which expressly prohibits that sort of thing.

These flack sites were, by and large, manned by Chinese. I could tell the difference because the Chinese personnel were a lot bigger. They were chanting and hooraying.

At the end of all of this parading about, which lasted a day or so, I was taken into a village where they held me for a while. In the village, a woman, who they informed me was a nurse, had the task to look after my knee.

She started poking around a little bit. She was just a young kid. She had on a white gown, but it became apparent that she didn't have a clue. She got out a band-aid and put it on the inside of my knee. That was the extent of the humane and lenient treatment given to me.

After the nurse finished, they took me into what appeared to be a town hall. About a hundred and fifty to two hundred Vietnamese filled this meeting room. They were seated on my right and my left. Right before me was a big portrait of Uncle Ho and Mao Tse Tung. A group of dignitaries sat at a table looking down at me. They had me sit on a low stool, the first of many stools I experienced in my stay up there. I never sat in a chair in all the years I spent in North Vietnam. The stool was an emblem of subservience. You were lower, and that's the message they wanted to convey.

I sat on this stool, and they began a tirade about how I'd been up there bombing and killing women and children, and now they were going to have a trial. So, they proceeded with their process. I didn't have a defense counsel, but I was allowed to speak if I wanted to. I gave my name, rank, service number and date of birth. They ultimately found me guilty, of course. When the verdict was given, there was an eruption of cheering and shouting from the assembled crowd. They sentenced me to death. They were going to take me out and execute me.

Then somebody interceded and said because of the humane and lenient treatment of the North Vietnamese government, they were going to spare my life. This came as great news to the crowd, and they cheered again. Everyone seemed happy. It was a big bunch of bullshit. It was a charade.

The night passed. The next day a jeep arrived with a couple of guys in tan uniforms. They were all business, and I knew they were the brown shirts, secret police, whatever you want to call them from downtown. They stuck me in the back of this little jeep. I was trussed up like a pig, and off we went to what I was certain was going to be Hanoi.

We drove through a bombing raid or two, and finally, we came to the approaches to what turned out to be the Paul Doumer Bridge. I had wiggled around to where I could adjust my blindfold a little and peek out beneath it, and I saw that we were going up on this bridge. It was a hell of a big structure which served both a railroad and highway bridge.

I think that when a train came across there wouldn't be room for vehicular traffic at the same time. We went across the bridge and into Hanoi. That became important to me later. They took me into the big Hoa Lo prison in Hanoi. I believe Hoa Lo in Vietnamese meant hell hole…and that was exactly what it was. The guys nicknamed it the Hanoi Hilton, but the Vietnamese knew it as the Hoa Lo prison.

It was right in the middle of downtown Hanoi. They took me in there in a jeep, dragged me out, and removed my blindfold. I was just standing out there without a blindfold, and it was getting dark. This was my second or third day in North Vietnam, and I still wore only my T-shirt and underwear shorts with no socks and no shoes. They let me wander around this little courtyard. There were people there, and the evening was becoming dark. The lanterns were lit, candles were lit, people were smoking and sitting on the stoops of these little huts, and it seemed they kind of forgot about me.

I'm out there thinking, jeez, if I had a place to go, I could go. I had to piss something fierce, so I went to a bush and peed there. Nobody said a word. Nobody paid one bit of attention to me, and I wondered for the longest time after, why in the world they were just ignoring me like that.

I found out later that the 19th of May had been a really bad day for a lot of people, not the least of which was the Navy. There had been six or eight aircraft losses that day. They were all stacked up in the interrogation room in there.

Eventually, maybe at ten that night, somebody finally showed up, grabbed me, and hauled me into what we came to know as the knobby room. It had great big knobs of plaster of Paris on the walls used for the dampening of sounds, so our screams of pain wouldn't be well heard throughout the prison. I didn't know that at the time of course. To me it appeared to be just an interesting presentation, a way to decorate a room.

There were some ropes in there, but there was no urinal, no pot, no nothing. There was just a table, a couple of chairs behind it, and a stool in front. They told me to sit on the stool. So, I sat down and waited. After some considerable period of time, maybe a half hour, forty-five minutes, in came what I took to be a couple of officers. I didn't know for sure if they were officers or not. They were wearing brown tunics with some kind of little epaulettes on them, but I didn't know what they were.

One of them spoke English, and he said, "What is your name?" I told them my name and my rank, major, my service number, and my date of birth.

Then he said, "What was your aircraft?" He started into these more specific questions. I kept repeating, name, rank, service number and date of birth.

Finally, he said, "That is not going to suffice. You're going to have to talk to us. Here are the camp regulations. They are very clear that all prisoners are to show a good attitude and answer all questions fully and honestly."

It was all bullshit. I told him I was only required to give him name, rank, and service number and date of birth by the Geneva Convention.

Then the guy literally exploded. He screamed, "The Geneva Convention does not apply!"

I asked why not, and he said, "You are criminals, this is an undeclared war, and you have attacked our country, and you are not going to be treated according to the Geneva Convention. You are going to talk to us, or we're going to punish you, because you are violating the camp regulations."

I didn't know what the hell to say. My knee was hurting pretty badly, and I was thinking to myself, "Geez, I really took a wrong turn here," but there was not a hell of a lot I could do.

He kept asking me questions particularly zeroing in on targeting, and that really bothered me. I had spent three years in Japan sitting alert to attack nuclear SIOP (Single Integrated Operations Plan) targets, and I was scared half to death they were going to start asking me about the nuclear targets. That was pretty dangerous stuff.

The truth was that nuclear targets were the least of my damn worries, but I didn't know that at the time. They didn't give a shit about the SIOP. I never once heard the SIOP mentioned in the six years I was there. But they really were concerned about targets in North Vietnam, specifically what the upcoming targets were going to be. It was just incredible how stupid this was. I had been on a target selection board in the 8th Wing. I was one of the three members of that group, the other two were Fighter Weapons School graduates. Though I'm not a FWS graduate, I was a distinguished crewman and had the credentials to serve on that committee, so Colonel Olds had put me on it. I knew the next twelve targets that the 8th Wing had targeted and was scheduled to strike.

There was no damn way I was going to tell them what those targets were. I just said to myself, "That ain't gonna come out of your mouth." We had seen that the North Vietnamese were moving SAMS and anti-aircraft guns around to different locations, and we didn't know why. The intelligence guys told us that, and they were doing it as a result of some kind of information they were getting.

I was about to find out the source of that intelligence. It was coming from the POWs, guys who were captured and were telling them what the next targets were. It became obvious that I was scheduled to be the next source.

I thought, "By God, I'm not going to do that."

About that time a very muscular guy came in. He was sort of small, but boy, I'll tell you, he was as strong as a sadistic ox. He knocked me off the stool, grabbed the ropes and proceeded to tie me up with them. He put manacles on me, with my hands behind my back. He put my feet in irons, with a metal bar running behind my ankles, perpendicular to my body, and they jammed a rag into my mouth to stifle screaming. Boy, he cinched up those ropes really tight.

Those two officers were sitting there, and one said, "When you're ready to talk, we're ready to listen."

That got pretty exciting. Then they put a rope around my neck, and I thought, "You know, I'm in real trouble here. I'm in more trouble than I've ever been in my life before. Jesus, I can't talk, and I can barely breath. One false move, and I'm dead."

I found out many years later in a book titled, "Inside Hanoi's Secret Archives," by Malcolm McConnell, that their deepest darkest secret was how many prisoners they killed in interrogation. I'm here to tell you that I went through that, and there was no question about it. They didn't have to make much of a mistake, and I was going to be a dead bunny.

It became obvious very quickly that I was in deep trouble. I wasn't going to tell them about those targets, but I was going to have to come up with something. I tried to knock myself out by beating my head on the floor, but that didn't work out. All I was doing was bloodying up my forehead and getting blood in my eyes.

I was thinking, "Lord, I need some help here." It flashed through my mind what Franklin Roosevelt said at his inauguration, "We have nothing to fear but fear itself." I thought that's true, but how the hell that ever chose to go through my mind at that particular time, I'll never know.

I believe a substantial number of POWs were killed in interrogation, and now they had me in their ropes. A lot of people had been seen on the ground after bailing out who just disappeared. I know now what happened to them. They went into the knobby room, and they died there. That was almost my fate, too. They were all business, and they were dead damn serious.

I could hear somebody screaming. I was sort of detached. I heard all this screaming, and I thought, "My God, somebody's really getting hurt."

When I realized the screaming was coming from me, it was scary as hell. I had never had anything like that happen to me before, and it went on for what seemed like hours. I don't think it was actually that long now. I think it was about forty-five minutes, maybe an hour.

I was a total mess. I shit in my pants. I pissed in them. After the beating, they attached a rope around my arms which were already tied together behind my back, elbows touching, and threw it over a hook in the ceiling. They hauled me up off the ground and began bouncing me up and down.

This dislocated my right shoulder. I had never, ever experienced any pain like that. I just didn't think that it was possible. I finally screamed that I would talk, and the officers came back in. I was semi-conscious. I was in and out. I have no idea how long that went on.

Finally, the little guy who had tied me up loosened the bindings a little bit. The releasing of the ropes caused the pain to be excruciating as the blood rushed back into my arms. The ropes had cut into my left arm. My right shoulder was dislocated, and I was a complete disaster. I was on my hands and knees. That was all I could do. I mean I couldn't stand. I couldn't do anything. I lost all circulation in my hands, my arms, and my feet. To this day, if it gets below fifty-five degrees both of my hands turn white. I don't have circulation in my hands at all. There are a whole bunch of us who don't.

After I came home, they finally came up with a surgical procedure that one could go through to alleviate the pain, but it isn't worth doing unless you are really and truly having problems. My arms go to sleep, my hands go to sleep just if I lie on them in bed. It's still scary now when that happens, and it was terrifying as hell at the time.

They pulled the rag out of my mouth. I had damn near strangled on it, and I threw up at that point. I was a basket case, crawling around on my hands and knees with blood everywhere. They told me to get back on the stool. I thought, "You gotta be shitting me. I can't get off the ground."

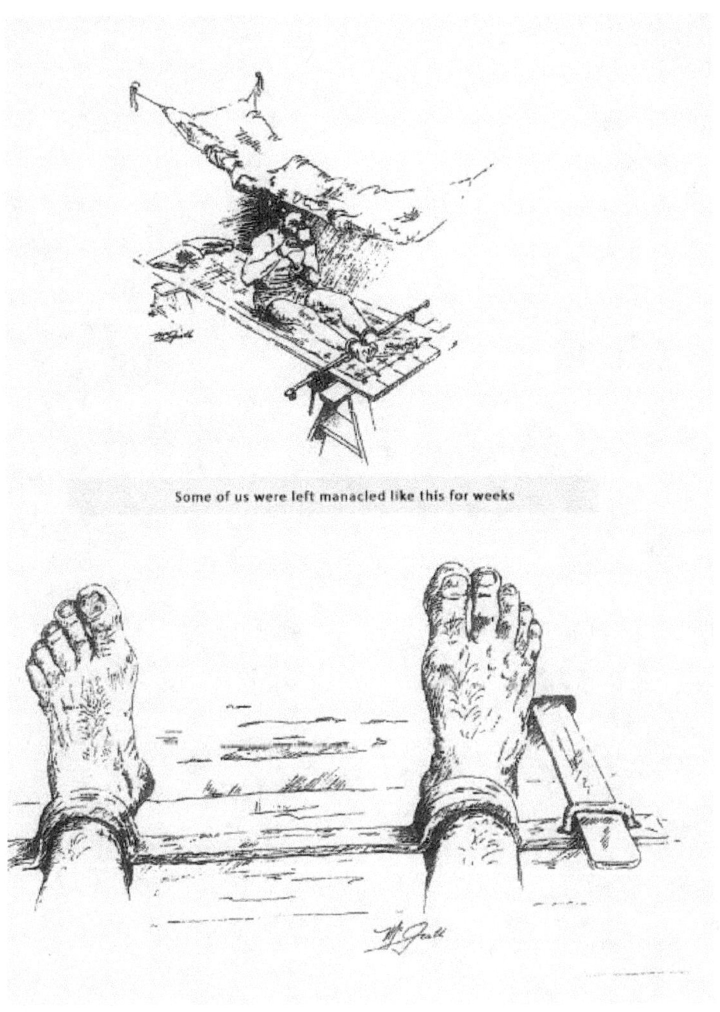

Some of us were left manacled like this for weeks

Courtesy of John M. McGrath, "Prisoner of War Six Years in Hanoi," Naval Institute Press, Annapolis, Maryland

Then the guy kicked me a couple of times in the balls just for emphasis, and that spurred me. I finally managed to crawl up on the stool. I sat there crying my eyes out. I had never ever been hurt like that before in my life.

Chapter 3 ★ The Information Game

THEY SAID, "OK, NOW YOU'RE GOING to talk to us, you son of a bitch. Tell us what the next target is."

I knew that I had to tell them something, or it would be back to the ropes, more torture. It was a fearsome situation, and I decided to feed them a line, hoping it would sell and without revealing any real knowledge I might have. I told them that the next target was going to be the Doumer Bridge, the one I crossed on my trip into Hanoi. In actual fact, I was pretty sure that it was no more the next target than I was King Kong. I told them it was the Paul Doumer Bridge, and I went to work on them.

They wanted to know when it was going to take place. I told them it would be in a couple of days. They wanted to know types of airplanes, altitudes, headings, the whole strike plan, and I gave them the whole nine yards. I constructed a raid in my head comprised of seventy-two F-105s and twenty-four F-4s. It was going to be the biggest raid of the war, and they were coming after the Paul Doumer Bridge. I gave them altitudes, airspeeds, bombs, and fuse settings. I just made up this enormous raid, and they said, "Now you're going to write all that down."

Hell, I couldn't even grasp anything after all of their tender ministrations to my hands, but I finally managed to grasp a pencil in the palm of my right hand, holding like a child might. I just gripped it clumsily and started to scratch out some words. It was totally illegible and wouldn't have meant a damned thing to anyone. However, those Vietnamese bastards' eyes really lit up when I talked about the Paul Doumer Bridge, and I could tell I was convincing them.

The more I realized that they were starting to believe me, the more my spirits went up. I thought, "Shit, I can outthink these fucking people, just barely," and they were buying into it. They ran out and got a couple of other interpreters to take notes. That was on what I think was the second full night I was in North Vietnam.

We actually did attack the Doumer Bridge but not until August. A substantial flight of F-105s came in, and the first guy put 2000 pounders right in the middle of the damn bridge. It fell in the river and that was the end of that. But my forecast was all bullshit, and that was how I got out of my first bout of torture. I just lied my way right out of it. I discovered that I was in the Department of Defense finishing school for liars, cheats, and thieves, and the name of the game was to get an "A." I was working my way toward it fast, telling these bastards about the Paul Doumer Bridge.

That was my welcome aboard as they kept me in that little room questioning me. My left arm is still damaged. I still have a lot of scars on it. There are also scars on my left leg from the irons going around my ankles. They had screws in them and they were not designed to fit around the ankles of a two-hundred-pound man. They were made for Asians weighing around one hundred pounds. But the bastards screwed them in anyway, and I have holes in my ankles from them and terrific scars on my left arm from the ropes.

In a day or so, the guy who had tied me up came in. My left arm was swollen to the size of my leg. He produced some mercurochrome and painted it, cleaning it a little. He grunted at me a couple of times and then left.

They kept constantly coming back and coming back, asking me more questions. Who was in my squadron, who was the commanding officer and on and on. This went on for eight days of stress and fear, and at the end of that time I was an absolute zombie. If anyone could have seen me then, they wouldn't have recognized me.

When I was in the middle of telling them about the Doumer Bridge they left, and I think they asked my back seater, Joe Milligan, about it. Apparently, he just kept saying, "I don't know, I don't know," but they didn't pressure him.

They beat the hell out of me, but they didn't press him, and finally I figured out that they thought that majors are supposed to know something, and lieutenants are not supposed to know anything. I guess that was their rationale.

Then they led me out to a primitive shower. On the wall above the shower head, someone had put a smiley face and scratched in, "Smile, you're on candid camera." I thought, "Well, at least somebody's got a sense of humor left."

My next stop on the highway of pain was Heartbreak Hotel which is a cell block with about eight cells in it. They were very small cubicles. In each one, there was a concrete block that had leg irons attached. They made me put my feet up into slots on the side next to the hall and then they clamped the irons on from the outside to lock me in. I sat there for seven or eight days. They kept interrogating me and running over my story.

I was paraded back in and asked me why the Americans hadn't attacked the Paul Doumer Bridge. I told them that the weather must have been bad. The necessity of maintaining an ongoing sales pitch of lies and creative fiction as a barrier against the threat of torture and possible death was terrifying. The whole thing was petrifying. I thought if they ever found out I was scamming them, I would never see another day.

The guards showed up one day and gave me a razor. I was allowed to go out and shave. I discovered a mirror there, and when I looked into it, I couldn't believe what I saw. I thought, "Man, you are really fucked up here."

I looked terrible. The open sore on my chin where I had been wounded by that clipboard was starting to heal, but I was having severe pressure points, mainly around my right ear. I started developing what I first thought were huge, damned boils. I had never experienced even a pimple to speak of as a kid, but now, here at the mercy of these sadists, all of us got these things. I believe they were stress induced.

They weren't really boils. They were carbuncles, and they were enormous, multi-headed things. It was the reaction to the constant threats, torture, and a result of the overall situation we were in. I got one on the outside of my right ear, and I couldn't believe the size of the damned thing. Some guys got them inside their noses and in their groins. We grew them everywhere. One time, Charley Rice counted one hundred and thirty-five of them on him. I'll tell you, that will get your undivided attention.

I was in pretty dismal shape. Occasionally, they showed up with some rice soup, and I ate what I could eat. The name of the game was that you had to eat in order to maintain some strength. We knew we had to get down whatever they brought us. They taught us that at survival school.

The main thing we constantly craved was water. It was May in Hanoi, and it was getting hot. We sure weren't in air-conditioned rooms, and it was stifling, like being locked in a malignant sauna. We would sit there dripping wet all day long, and we just couldn't get enough water. They gave us a quart in the morning and a quart in the afternoon. It was all boiled water, so when you got it, it was still hot. I'd go through that damned water like it was the nectar of the gods. Any potable liquid was consumed to the last drop. When they gave us soup, not an iota of it was left when we were finished.

I had a mat. I had my red pajamas, the long sleeve official uniform. I had a couple of them, actually. They issued me some gray shorts, a couple of frayed tops, a tin cup, an old toothbrush, a little bar of soap that I imagine they made out of lard, and a mosquito net. Thank God we had those nets.

The guards would come in and say to me, "Roll up." That meant I was to put all my stuff into one end of my rice mat and get ready to move. Then I would be blindfolded, and they would start pushing me along toward some other room. That was pretty exciting, too, just trying to blindly find my way going up and down stairs and around corners. I was continually banging and bumping into things.

While I was in the Heartbreak Hotel, there were people coming and going, and the guards started yelling, "Bow." I soon learned that I had to get up and bow every time they opened the little peephole and looked in my cell.

They didn't like the way I bowed, either. It seemed that I wasn't doing it exactly right. I didn't bow deeply enough for them. I don't think I ever did bow quite the way they wanted. Those bastards would come in and really slap guys around to get them to bow. This went on until after Ho died in September of 1969. I was shot down in May of 1967. So, for almost two-and-one-half years, we bowed all that time while I was there. Then, after a while, they told us to stop bowing.

That was my welcome aboard. It was as dramatic as hell, because I would hear other guys yelling and screaming when they were being tortured, and I thought, "Son of a bitch, what the hell did I get into here?"

If any of us made any mention of the Geneva Convention, they just unloaded on us. The most sensitive thing to them was to keep us from talking to each other. They start talking to us about that. They said, "If we catch you communicating, we will beat the shit out of you."

Of course, we were always communicating in Heartbreak Hotel, but if a guy was down looking under the doors, and the guards caught him, they would come in and beat the hell out of him. I'll tell you when you are in that kind of situation, you are pretty easily intimidated.

Chapter 4★ The Mission

FLYING FIGHTER COMBAT MISSIONS DURING THE Vietnam war was unlike any air war, before or since. There was a surreal air of normalcy to it that decried the deadliness of the undertaking. The crews got up, went to work much like other Americans in more peaceful times and locals. They flew their missions, debriefed, and then went home or to the officers' club for a drink.

Unlike their warrior brethren on the ground in jungles and rice paddies, the fighter pilots and crewmen rarely showed up in hospitals with treatable wounds or at pickup points in body bags. They just flew away and from time to time, some didn't come back.

A military nurse working in Vietnam once told me that she thought the young ones, meaning the soldiers, were the only ones who got hurt. From her point of view, she was correct, since those were the only ones she ever saw. Her skepticism about losses in our squadrons was disconcerting though, because in terms of deaths and capture, we suffered much higher losses than almost any ground unit.

There were no catastrophic losses of formations as had occurred in World War II where a combat tour was twenty-five missions, and those missions were deadly indeed. In the Southeast Asia air war, especially over North Vietnam, there was just a steady and deceptive loss rate that didn't make an impression on those who were not personally involved in it.

The full impact was often not felt even by those in the combat squadrons, because the men had not come there as a unit. There were constant, ongoing replacements of those lost or who had finished their tours of duty. These men were replaced in relatively uneventful turnovers of new crew members from the stateside training programs, and the "old heads" tended not to really get to know the FNGs, the fucking new guys.

Men became hardened and numbed to the ongoing reports of losses and did not grieve long, even when the one lost was a friend. There was always tomorrow and another mission to fly.

The airplanes were missed only by the ground crews.

When a fighter aircraft went down, it was replaced in a day or so by another identically painted, camouflaged replacement. The process was seamless, and nobody who was not involved in the handling of these craft would ever even notice.

Our tours of duty were either one year or the completion of one hundred missions over North Vietnam, whichever came about first. Some squadron mathematician worked it out at one point that we were losing an average of about one aircraft for every 200 missions flown over North Vietnam. That didn't sound so bad until it was pointed out that in a 100-mission tour, each of us had a fifty-fifty chance of being shot down. When that occurred over North Vietnam, the chances of being killed or taken prisoner were excellent.

We generally flew one of three types of missions to North Vietnam. One was a strike mission, to deliver bombs on the specific targets allowed by Lyndon Johnson and his band of bureaucrats back in Washington DC. The reasoning for determining which targets were allowed to be hit and which were off limits was incomprehensible to the men tasked to fly and occasionally die to accomplish their designated duties.

The airfields that were home to the Soviet built MiG fighters, for example, were forbidden as targets for most of the war, even though we could see enemy aircraft moving about on the ground below us. We were not allowed to strike them in any way until they climbed up to kill us. Nonetheless, we went out day after day and did what they told us to do.

A second mission was armed reconnaissance, which involved flying a particular route. The routes were color coded such as "Red Route" or "Blue Route" or some other regularly scheduled land target area. These were flown against targets of opportunity, primarily trucks moving equipment south to the ground battle areas or anti-aircraft guns.

The third mission that we flew on a regular basis was MiG CAP (Combat Air Patrol), against MiG-21 or MiG-17 fighters that would come to shoot down our fighters carrying the bombs. This was also known as escort or cover for other bomb carrying fighters. At times, the MiG Cap fighters were the same type aircraft (F-4 Phantoms) as those that were carrying bombs north. They would be configured with air-to-air missiles for CAP missions instead of bombs, but an aircraft and crew that went north with bombs one day might be tasked for MiG CAP the next.

On the twentieth of May 1967, I was on the schedule as the ground spare to "fly if needed," for a flight led by Colonel Robin Olds as MiG Cap for a raid on the Northeast Railroad. Olds was the flight leader, Bill Kirk was his wingman, flying Number 2, Bob Pardo was 3, and Ron Catton was flying Number 4. I was the ground spare tasked to start engines, taxi out, and be available in case someone aborted.

We briefed the mission, and Olds' idea of the briefing was, "Just keep me in sight. We're going up, and we're gonna chase the F-105s in, then we'll be looking for MiGs." The whole name of the game for the wingmen was to keep Olds in sight as best they could.

There was an emotional factor to the mission because several people had left their leaders or mission the moment a shot was fired. In some cases, when a MiG showed up, a few of the wingmen had abandoned their flight leaders.

Unfortunately, a man I knew well was one of them. I'll call him Jim X. He had been shot at a couple of times and had abandoned his leader each time. In private, I told him, "You simply cannot leave your leader like that. You have to stay with him. Your job is to protect his six o'clock."

He said, "Yeah but the damn bullets were going by. What was I supposed to do?"

I told him, "Well you're going to stay right there with him and try to protect him." That didn't seem to make too much sense to a former KC-135 pilot, but it made a lot of sense to me, because that was the way I had been trained to fight.

I was particularly intent on staying with Col. Olds in all cases and was determined not to allow any possibility of stigma attached to my courage or competence during the flight. Like most fighter pilots, I would have rather died than been considered a coward or let down my brother warriors. I still feel that way.

I guess I should say that the combat formation that we used in those days was Air Force air-to-air doctrine at the time. Unfortunately, it was a factor in helping me lose six years of my life and costing me a lot of pain.

The Air Force still trained and operated in a method of flying air combat formation called Fluid Four, comprised to two two-ship elements that was, by 1967, as obsolete as the dodo. When maneuvering, the basic two-ship fighting element flew in a formation called a fighting wing, which required that the wingman stay in position back at an angle of about sixty degrees to the leader and to stay there regardless of what the leader did.

This antiquated concept was adopted during or just after the Korean War many years earlier, where kills were made with guns and every fighter had only a single seat. The wingman was expected to hang in on his leader and clear the sky behind them while the leader shot down MiGs. The wingman often achieved this goal by getting himself shot off the element lead's wing, while the leader lived to fight another day.

With the adoption of the two-seat F-4 Phantom as the primary air to air fighter, this formation was seriously flawed. Phantoms had a back seater with mirrors to help him see behind, and he was able to clear behind at least as well as a single seat fighter flying fighting wing had been able to do previously.

The Navy, always well ahead of the Air Force in air combat doctrine and training, had long since gone to a different formation called the "Loose Deuce." This had the element of two fighters operating independently and supporting each other without having their capabilities degraded by the fighting wing formation. The Air Force adapted similar tactics years later.

I went to work getting some experience there. I flew my first ten missions in Route Pack One in southern North Vietnam. Eventually, I worked my way up into the number three, element leader spot. They didn't have many leaders, and I had a good bit of experience. I had around 200 hours in the F-4 when I became a combat flight lead. There were very few of us in that status. I was in the 433rd Squadron, and Fred Crow was my ops officer.

Our squadron commander, however, had no more business being a squadron commander than a pig going to war. He didn't have any experience. He didn't want to be there. He was scared to death.

Bill Kirk was in the wing with a bunch of guys from Bentwaters, a U.S. air base in England. We called them the Bentwaters mafia. Robin had brought a lot of experience with him from Bentwaters, and that was good.

We started flying, and a lot of the missions were at night. There were three fighter squadrons there, the 497th, the 555th (Triple Nickel), and the 433rd (Satan's Angels). I started flying combat missions, gaining experience and learning the ropes.

On one occasion, I was flying in a flight of four on a MiG suppression mission chasing F-105s, going to strike the Thai Nguyen steel mill. For two or three days we weather aborted, but finally we got a go. The weather was still dog shit, but we went up there.

The first flight of four of the escort F-4s was being led by a major out of my squadron, and I was the flight lead for the second flight of four. We were in support of the F-105 strike force led by Bob, "Double R," Scott, from Korat or Takhli. His call sign was "Crab" lead. We got as far as approaching the Black River, and I heard this voice say, "Hey, Crab, when are you going to make a weather decision?"

I told my back seater, "Boy I'm sure glad that isn't one of us talking. If I were Colonel Scott, I'd tell them to shut up."

But what Scott said very reasonably was, "Well, I'm going to fly a little bit further, then I'll make a decision."

We went a little bit further, and this same voice said, "Hey, Crab Lead, when are you going to make the decision on the weather?"

This time, a little more irritably, Scott said, "When I get to the Red, I'll make a decision."

We kept going, and all of a sudden, I saw a flash off to my left, and I heard somebody call out, "There are MiGs down there."

My back seater said, they're not MiGs, they're F-4s. I called, and said, "They're F-4s," thinking they were probably recce birds coming back out from the target area. I saw two more and realized they were fighters and not recce birds.

Then Scott called the whole thing off, and we went back home. I was in the last flight of four following the F-105s. As it turned out, the guy leading the first flight of F-4s, also from my squadron as MiG suppression, had abandoned the mission and the F-105s that he was supposed to be escorting. He just took off and bugged out. He didn't like the weather, so he left Colonel Scott and the F-105s without his support.

When I got on the ground, Fred Crow, my ops officer, was at the foot of the ladder and he said, "Did you leave the 105s before they called the weather abort?"

I replied, "Hell no. Of course, I didn't."

He said, "OK." The leader of the first flight should have done that, and Colonel Olds sent him home really quick as he should have.

Colonel Olds had a small issue with me as well, but not enough to get me sent home. When I first arrived in Vietnam, I ran right into Robin Olds. He was the 8th TFW commander. He welcomed me and promptly told me to lose weight.

I said, "I work at that all the time, Colonel," which I have, and which I do. My weight has been a problem all my life, as long as I can remember.

The next day, we went back up again, and this time I was flying the lead flight of four. We were supporting Colonel Scott again. We got up fairly close to the target, and the weather was just terrible. We had no more business up there than the man in the moon. There was just a bunch of airplanes milling around. SAMs were going by and the RHAW (Radar Homing and Warning) system was squawking. I finally told my guys to just turn the things off. We are staying here no matter what. We were in pod formation.

We went all the way to the target, turned over the target and came back out. Finally, Scott called and said, "Buick are you still there?"

I answered him, "Yes sir, I'm right here."

"OK, good." About a minute later, he said we were clear to break off.

I called back, "Crab, I will be taking you to the tanker."

He chuckled and said, "OK."

I took him to the tanker, and then asked if we were cleared off.

He said we were.

Then, he called Olds and said, "Well you found somebody who had a little bit of guts anyhow."

Olds didn't like that at all. He really didn't like the fact that one of his pilots had badly embarrassed the wing and him the day before.

It was interesting flying combat up there and seeing some people who just folded up under the pressure. We had more than one who did that, but this was an occasion I remember well.

I'll never forget the day the order came down to attack the Thai Nguyen steel mill, and we got the pictures out. I was scheduled to lead the first flight of four escorting the F-105s. My flight commander was a kid by the name of Tommy McGay or McGee, something like that.

He came into the room, looked at the pictures, and said, "My God, that's a Silver Star mission."

It hadn't occurred to me before that, but I soon realized that there were a lot of guys who were there just for career progression, for enhanced promotions, or to get medals. I guess I was just naive. I was focused on flying my one hundred missions to North Vietnam and finishing that tour.

What I had really wanted to do after that was to go down to Cam Rahn Bay in South Vietnam, so I could see what it was like to fly close support with troops down there. That was my game plan, but it got cut short on the 20th of May 1967, when I was shot down.

We all started engines at Ubon that fateful day, going through our after-start checks and confirming the status of our armament. We each were carrying four radar guided AIM-7 (Aerial Intercept Missile-7) Sparrow missiles and four heat seeking AIM-9 Sidewinder missiles. The Sidewinders were checked on the ground by moving a flashlight in front of the seeker heads of the missiles. There would be a growl detected in the pilot's headset by each missile from the heat of the flashlight. The Sparrows were checked by a switch process in the air.

The flight took off while I waited on the ground with my engines running. Almost immediately after that, Bill Kirk called that he had a BLC (Boundary Layer Control) light. The first thing to do in that case is to put the gear and flaps back down and get on the ground as soon as possible, because you have a potentially serious problem. He declared an emergency and landed.

JACK VAN LOAN & JOE MILLIGAN

Olds called and said, "Jack, take off and join us," so I did. As I was joining up on the left side, Robin called for a channel change. When we changed channels, my radio started cycling, making the clicking noise that indicates the radio is in the process of changing channels. Normally this lasts a few seconds, goes off, and then you can communicate.

Sometimes a radio would take longer than normal to channelize, and during this time, as the clicking sound goes on, there is no communication. You can't hear anything, and you cannot transmit. Once in a great while, the radio never completes the change, and the pilot is then without means to hear any transmission or to transmit, effectively deaf and mute.

Olds kept looking over at me and signaling with his hands what channel I was supposed to be on, and I was giving him an OK, I'm right here, but it continued cycling. Finally, my radio channeled in. He said, "Two, do you read me?"

I answered, "Yes sir, I'm right here."

"What's the problem?" he asked.

I told him that the radio was working now, and we proceeded. This was a mistake that was to cost me six years of my life and also that of my back seater. I should never have gone into North Vietnam with an unreliable radio, and I regret that I did so very much now.

Anyhow, we were in support of a strike mission against the Northeast Railroad, and we were flying MiG CAP for the F-105 strike force lead by Major Phil Gast. We met at the KC-135 refueling anchor track over the South China Sea. I think it was Yellow Anchor, but I can't remember for sure now. We rendezvoused with the tankers along with the F 105s out there over the ocean, and everybody got refueled.

When we finished refueling and were approaching the coast, there were sixteen F-105s, four flights of four down below us. Major Gast, later General Gast, then said something that was to me incomprehensible. He said, "Watch it guys, it's very quiet."

Talk about superfluous comments on the radio, that's it. It's almost like, "You see any bogies?"

I thought to myself, "What do you think I'm doing, taking a nap?"

Nonetheless, he pressed on, and then all of a sudden, it wasn't quiet at all. We were jumped by a whole bunch of MiGs. I mean there were MiGs everywhere. Two of them started to roll in on Gast down low, and to my dismay, my radio started cycling again at that precise point. It just kept click, click, clicking.

Olds punched off his fuel tank, but I never heard him call to do that. We all had centerline 600-gallon tanks. I saw his leave, so I pulled up and punched mine off too.

Then I rolled it back over, pushed the stick forward, and I saw two MiGs on Major Gast. I put my nose down and fired a Sparrow at them in boresight. The moment the Sparrow went off, they turned into me, and I pulled back up. I was trying to get back on Robin's wing. He was accelerating away from me, and I was trying to catch up.

Then, I saw a 37-millimeter cannon ball streaking by me. I was trying like hell to accelerate and catch up to Olds. The next thing I knew, every light in the cockpit came on. I could feel the bullets hitting me. I had two overheat lights and two fire lights. I turned back to the right toward the coast, because I knew the airplane was mortally damaged.

About that time, the stick froze. The thought went through my mind about friends of mine in the F-100 who had had trouble with the autopilot system. The stick would freeze, and they'd screw around with it for a while, and then they'd hit the ground. We lost a number of guys that way.

I always told myself that if the stick ever froze, I was out of there. I wasn't going to stay with it. I told Joe Milligan, my back seater, "Joe, we're hit."

He said, "How bad?"

I replied, "Real bad." I knew he was back there spring loaded to the eject position. I said, "Get out," and waited about two nanoseconds before I pulled on the handle between my legs.

Joe, by the way, stayed in the Air Force when we came home. He went to Rutgers University and then to veterinary school. He became a veterinarian and eventually the head vet in the Air Force, a full colonel. A very good guy and a very, very good pilot. He deserved a lot better than to be sitting in my back seat that day.

DEPARTMENT OF THE AIR FORCE
HEADQUARTERS 8TH TACTICAL FIGHTER WING (PACAF)
APO SAN FRANCISCO, 96304

22 MAY

Dr. and Mrs Wendel L. Van Loan
2570 West, 22d Ave, Eugene, Oregon

Dear Doctor and Mrs Van Loan

It is with deep personal feeling that I write this letter of circumstances concerning the missing status of your son, Major Jack L. Van Loan. Your anxiety is sincerely shared by each and everyone of us who know and worked with him.

Major Van Loan was flying as Aircraft Commander in a flight of F-4C aircraft on a strike mission over North Vietnam, and his aircraft was hit by a MIG aircraft while engaged in aerial combat. Moments later two parachutes were observed descending. It appears that Major Van Loan and his co-pilot ejected safely from their aircraft. The weather was clear and the terrain mountainous. Major Van Loan and his co-pilot were equipped with survival equipment. Due to the hazardous location, aerial or ground search could not be made.

Please accept my deepest sympathy during this trying period. I assure you that everything possible is being done to determine your son's status. I will immediately pass on to you any additional information which I may receive. The incident happened at approximately 3:30 P.M., 20 May 1967.

Sincerely

Robin Olds

ROBIN OLDS, Colonel, USAF
Commander

LETTER TO JACK'S PARENTS FROM HIS COMMANDER

Chapter 5★ Little Vegas

AFTER THE EIGHT-DAY WELCOME-ABOARD session, I was pretty badly beaten up both physically and emotionally. They managed to punch a hole into my ankle, into the bone there. That got infected, and I couldn't put any weight on it. The pain was a constant, throbbing excruciation. My arm was infected from where the ropes had cut into it, so I was pretty much incapacitated. As I mentioned, they put me into a place the guys called Heartbreak Hotel. I had been there about eight or nine days when the guards came along and told me to roll up my stuff. So off I went carrying what little I had: a rice mat, tin cup, toothbrush, a little bit of toothpaste and a couple pair of T- shirts, made of rough, gray material.

I was blindfolded, so I kept bumping into things and falling down as they prodded me along. It was a Laurel and Hardy act just trying to get me from the Heartbreak Hotel to Little Vegas. Little Vegas was named that because different wings of the Hanoi Hilton were named for casinos: the Stardust, the Mint, and so forth, hotels in Las Vegas.

They finally stopped me and took the blindfold off. I was standing at a door which they opened and shoved me through into a small cell. I met my first roommate, a Navy Lieutenant JG (Junior Grade) named Read Mecleary. He had been shot down in an A-4, and when he ejected, he broke both knees when his legs wrapped around the seat. He could roll over but that was about it. He couldn't walk at all.

They put me in there to look after Read. His knees were in really bad shape. I started working on him, massaging him and just trying to get some circulation going. It was marvelous to have a roommate, the first good thing after my shoot down, even though we both were in constant pain. Mecleary had been tortured but not quite as severely as I had.

The North Vietnamese didn't beat up the junior officers as severely as they did the more senior officers. They really came down hard on them. We called them the chiefs, and the rest of us were the Indians.

They came after the chiefs on a daily basis but by and large left us Indians alone as long as we didn't get into trouble. Unfortunately, that happened on a fairly regular basis.

After a few days, I was let out to get some food or something, and I heard a hoarse whisper. A voice identified the speaker as Fred Crow, who had been my ops officer in the 433rd squadron "Satan's Angels" at Ubon Air Base in Thailand. He had been shot down before I had. He identified himself and asked me how I was. I let him know that my knee was hurt, my leg and arm were infected from the torture, but I was getting by all right.

He asked me who I was living with, and I told him Mecleary. This was passed in clandestine, whispered conversations. He also told me how the tap code worked. You had to know the tap code to be able to communicate from one cell to the next.

The cells there didn't have common walls. They had offset them in such a clever manner that there were no common walls in Little Vegas at all. Because of that, you couldn't go up to the wall and start tapping and expect the guy next door to hear you. The only common wall was the back wall and to pound on that would have alarmed the guards.

There was a good bit of whispering going on. In order to have security, you had to lie down on your belly on the floor and look under the door to see the guard's shoes coming, then jump up before he could open the door. It was difficult to be hopping up and down like that with bad knees. Read couldn't do anything at that time, so what little communication we had was done by me. It was really a challenge.

Read was from Connecticut, and as I write this, is finishing up a career flying with American Airlines, as a lot of the guys did. Read has been a captain for many years now.

The first thing he asked me, as soon as we met, was how long I thought we were going to be there. I thought to myself, should I tell this guy the truth or not? I didn't want to do that, because I was concerned that we were going to be there for a long time. I had given it a lot of thought.

I decided that I just couldn't tell Read what I really thought. I was convinced by then that it was going to take somebody other than Lyndon Johnson as President to end the war. It was my perception that he had absolute contempt for the Vietnamese, and though I didn't really know it at that time, I suspected that the North Vietnamese had the same view of Lyndon Johnson.

If I had answered that question truthfully, I would probably have said, "Five more years." Then I thought, if I say that to him, I'm probably going to destroy any morale he may have left. So, I said, "Well, McNamara told us the boys would be home for Christmas, so it ought to be around then." I didn't believe that for an instant.

I thought we had to have another President before things would be stabilized enough to get us out, and sure enough, that's exactly what happened. Then the next President, Richard Nixon, started the Vietnamization program, so we sat there for another four years while the U.S. had a very slow drawdown in order to "withdraw with honor." I didn't know whether the damned war would ever end.

My left ankle and leg were badly infected. The guards finally showed up with what passed for a doctor. He gave me some pills and eventually they gave me some penicillin.

Their idea of giving penicillin was sort of a shock. They brought this big needle, jammed it in my arm and pushed like hell. My God, I'd never had that kind of instant burning pain before ever, period. That was their idea of "taking care of it." They gave me a couple of penicillin shots that were worse than the infection. Eventually, after weeks and weeks, my wounds slowly began to heal. In the meantime, all I could do in those days was hop like a bunny.

They made a point of not letting us out where we could see each other. They were trying like hell to keep us from communicating. They were constantly peeking in the little window, and then you'd have to get up and bow to them.

The Vietnamese had a sort of "siesta hour." They took a nap every day around 1 or 2 o'clock for an hour or so. That was when we would get in a little quiet communicating. The guards finally figured out what we were doing, and they'd come around to try to catch us.

If you got caught, it was bad business. You got jerked out, and you got to see the Rabbit or the Rat (the infamous rodents). Those guys were sadistic bastards. If they got you, it was hurting time again. Boy, you were back in the ropes, and then you had to start telling them who the SRO (Senior Ranking Officer) was and what he was saying.

The SRO was God, no question about it. That was the only way we could ever maintain discipline. Whoever the senior guy was, regardless of the service branch, he was the man with authority. The guys got that through their heads real quick like. It didn't make any difference whether they were Navy or Air Force.

I think that might have created a problem—sometimes a little resentment on the part of the Air Force guys. The Navy promoted officers to lieutenant commander faster than we promoted people to major (the equivalent Air Force rank). There might be a couple of guys living together and the Air Force guy might have had more commissioned time, but the Navy guy had date of rank on him. However, that never created any serious problems that I was ever aware of. Charlie Southwick and I lived together for years. We were about the same age. He was senior to me, though I had a more commissioned time than he did.

One day I was out there doing my hopping around routine. When I came around the corner, the guards had gotten themselves fucked up, and I literally bumped into CAG Jim Stockdale. We call him CAG (Commander Air Group), or Sir, or Admiral. He is an absolute hero of mine. He is one of the toughest, smartest, most articulate men I have ever met. His wife, Sybil is right up there with him for my respect. He later ran for Vice President with Ross Perot.

However, that day, he was white as a sheet. His hair was prematurely gray, and he had on old, faded prison garb. He looked like a ghost. He mumbled something like "hello," and the guards started yelling at us, so we went our separate ways. I didn't see him again until a little while before we were released, and we started having stand-up staff meetings. Jerry Denton,

Stockdale, and Robby Risner, all those old guys were there. You felt like you were in with the legends.

Somebody whispered to me that Stockdale was the SRO, and the North Vietnamese did their dead level best to keep him as incommunicado as they could. It was hard to keep him out of the communications chain, but they did a pretty good job of it. When he was out of the mainstream, Jerry Denton took over.

Stockdale was out there flying top cover the night the destroyers…Maddox and Turner Joy…were ostensibly attacked by North Vietnamese patrol boats. I've talked to CAG at length about that, and he believes that there were no torpedo boats out there at all. He was right over the top of them, and Charlie Southwick was his wingman.

Later the Rabbit came around, I don't remember exactly when, and told Stockdale he was going to be in a movie as the bad guy, and they would be the good guys. Jim said, "No, I'm not going to make any movie or do anything like that."

The Rabbit said, "Then you will be punished. We will make you do it."

Stockdale said, "Have at it."

So, they tortured him, put him back in the ropes. He was in the ropes seventeen times during the years that he was in prison. I honest to God don't know how he did it, and he has a leg that has atrophied at the knee as a result. He limped around on his bad leg. They would break it, then they would just break it again.

Jesus, he went through excruciating pain. You could hear him screaming all over the prison. It was blood chilling.

Rabbit put him in the ropes again, and pretty soon Stockdale was screaming, "I yield, I yield, I give up, I'll do it." They sent him off to shave for his movie appearance, and I'm here to tell you I'm just not this tough at all. I couldn't have done this. He took the razor blade out of the razor they had given him, and he just shredded himself, sliced up his face. He turned around and had blood running everywhere. The guard let out a scream and went running off to get the Rabbit.

When the Rabbit came back, he looked at him and said, calmly, "You will heal, and I will be back." They threw him back in his cell with a rag to clean himself up a bit. A doctor came along and painted him up with mercurochrome. He looked like an Indian on the warpath.

Sure enough, he did heal, and sure enough, the Rabbit came back.

He said, "Now we'll make the movie."

The CAG replied, "I'm not making any movie."

"But you said you would."

"Yeah, when you tortured me," he said, "go ahead."

They put him back in the ropes, and again he got beat up really bad. Finally, he said, "I give up, I give up." This time when they put him out to shave and get cleaned up, the Rabbit told the guard to watch him.

Jim was leaning over to wash his face off, and he took the razor and gave himself a reverse Mohawk. He sliced up his scalp, so he's got hair and blood and skin coming down his face. The guard went crazy, and he's screaming his lungs out.

Back came the Rabbit.

The Rabbit looked at Stockdale and said, "You can wear a hat."

When the Rabbit went off to get the hat they left him in this room, sitting on a stool. He picked the stool up and beat his eyes shut. I'm here to tell you, that's beyond me. I wouldn't have had the imagination or the courage to do that.

He set an example for us of resistance for us that, in my opinion, saved lives.

Years later, we were at the White House and Admiral Zumwalt was the head of my table. When there was a break, I went over to the Admiral and sat down with him. I said, "Admiral, your man CAG Stockdale, in my opinion, richly deserves the Medal of Honor."

Zumwalt looked at me with those big bushy eyebrows and just said one word, "Why?"

I told him the story about the Rabbit. He said, "Thank you very much, Colonel."

He went back to the Pentagon and evidently wrote a memo to his staff to get hold of this Lt. Col. Van Loan and get the quotes on Stockdale.

Nobody did anything. They screwed up and dropped the ball. Fifteen months later, I was up in Oregon visiting my parents and the phone rang. It was Red McDaniel, my long-time cellmate, now a Navy captain working in the Pentagon.

He said, "The heat's really on."

"What's the matter?" I replied.

He said, "Remember that night you told Zumwalt about Stockdale?"

"Sure."

"Well, he's now left the Chief of Naval Operations job, and he's got this transition office where he's reviewing all his papers. He came across this memo, and nobody had bothered to do anything about it. He got the Navy personnel guy in there, and he got another three star who was in there. You could hear him all around the Pentagon E-ring screaming at them he was so mad."

They came to Red and said they couldn't find me in Tucson. They gave Red a direct order, "You find him."

Red said, "I think he's on vacation."

"We don't care where he is, you find him and get him to call."

I was on my way back to the National War College, and these guys were going to send a plane to haul me back to Washington and have my wife and kids drive alone.

I said, "No, I'm not going to do that. Hell, you guys have waited this long, you can wait until I get there."

I got to Arlington at the end of the holidays, and there was a Navy staff car sitting there waiting for me. They hauled me down to the Pentagon. I wrote it up and Stockdale got the Medal of Honor (MOH) which he richly deserved.

President Gerry Ford presented it to him sometime later.

And that was the story of Stockdale, the Rabbit and the MOH. CAG deserved it and so did Robinson Risner. Those guys saved lives through their unbelievable heroism. There are no two ways about it.

So that was my introduction into Little Vegas, and I was there until around August. About that time, they packed us up and took us to the power plant one night.

Chapter 6★ The Power Plant

HO CHI MINH HAD ANNOUNCED THAT he was going to chain the prisoners to lucrative targets. One night, we were blindfolded and taken down a darkened little passageway into a room. The room had obviously been an office building, but it had seen better days. It had a naked light bulb hanging there and there was damage to the walls. There had obviously been a lot of bombing around there.

The next morning a guard came around and opened up the door. We could have kicked that door right off the hinges, so it was obviously a temporary deal. When I went to get food, I looked around. We were in the office section of a large building of about seven rooms. The other part of the building was a foundry, and it was all bombed out.

I walked down into a small courtyard. When I looked up, I could see that we were right next to the large, electrical power plant in down-town Hanoi. I could have hit a wedge shot and knocked it right to the edge of the building. We were that close. I went back to our room and told Mecleary, who still couldn't get around for shit, "Read, we're right at ground zero. We're at the power plant." I described what I had seen.

Then the guards came along and startled us half to death. They opened up the shuttered windows, and I found myself looking right out into the street. I mean there was a road right there. I could spit right onto the street, and I could stick my head through the bars. As you probably know, if you can stick your head through an opening, you can get your body through it too. The bars were clearly cosmetic, there just for looks.

With the blinds open, we watched people going by. There were gunners that came by when they changed shifts at the flack site down the street. Civilians were wandering around, looking in the windows at us. It was obvious that they meant for us to be seen. They intended for the word to get out that we were there, right at the power plant.

When Mecleary saw where we were, he said, "Well now that they know we are here, they won't bomb us."

I told him, "Read, I hate to disappoint you, but we're losing five hundred kids a week in South Vietnam. I guarantee you that if they want to take out that power plant, they are coming in to get it regardless of whether we're here or not."

I don't think he ever believed me, but sure enough, they did come in and bomb it. They took it out while there were POWs still there. It was a pretty exciting day.

What the North Vietnamese had done to protect that power plant was unbelievable. They had built a cement wall around it with a six-foot-thick base. I saw it when we were allowed to go into the power plant to get water. Later they put a lot of other POWs there. I can't remember who they were, or who the SRO was either, but there was rubble all around the place.

Then the Vietnamese shot down a couple more Navy guys. They brought them in there and beat the crap out of them to get them to talk about the television guided bomb the Navy had. This TV bomb had to have contrast to work well, so the Vietnamese proceeded to paint the whole damn area and buildings black. They used this fish-based paint on everything including the power plant.

Then the North Vietnamese came up with something that just cracked us up. This is the honest-to-God's truth. We almost died laughing. They decided a better idea would be to work on getting good intelligence on when the fighters were coming in and then put smoke pots out there. That's what they did.

They put hundreds of smoke pots all around the plant. When they thought that the fighter bombers would be coming, they lit off all the pots. The smoke rose to about one story above the ground. The power plant was a five-story black building that stuck out of the top of the white cloud of smoke from the pots. It was a perfect contrast. They had constructed a perfect target.

The wall was five feet thick at the base and tapered up to about two feet thick four or five stories up. A couple of TV bombs came into the top of the power plant, and the whole thing collapsed from the concussion inside there.

The guys next door to that power plant heard a tremendous explosion. They knew it had been bombed, but it didn't bother them at all. The whole thing collapsed from the inside of this big protective wall they had built around it. We couldn't stop laughing. How they could manage to do something like that was beyond me, but they did it.

I had been at Heartbreak Hotel, then Little Vegas, then we were there at the power plant for about a month. They next moved us to the Plantation. I was off to the Plantation, having no idea what these places were. The Plantation was an old French place the North Vietnamese made into an impromptu prison.

Chapter 7★ The Zoo

IN APRIL OF 1968, I HAD managed to offend the North Vietnamese badly by telling them that there was going to be an invasion probably around Vinh. I told them that the Chinese would come in from the North, and the U.S. would invade the South, and the North Vietnamese would go to Laos. As Dick Stratton later told me, my bullshit efforts obviously pushed them too far and too hard.

They got pretty upset about that and told me that I was in deep shit. One day they came in and told me, Read McCleary, and Jim Bailey to pack up, that we were moving. So, we bundled up all our crap and they put us in the back of a truck, blindfolded, of course, all tied up and off we went.

The next thing we knew, they ushered us into a whitewashed room in what turned out to be the building called the Pigsty in the Zoo. We had graduated to the big time. The Zoo was where they kept the most troublesome POWs. It was the hard rock slam from the word go.

We started the new digs by meeting the Rat. He was there to welcome us aboard and tell us that we were just criminals. He told us about the rules and to obey them, or we were going to be punished severely. I was inclined to believe him.

The Zoo name came from the fact that the Vietnamese were constantly coming around and opening the peepholes to peer in. It was just like looking at animals in a cage, so the guys named the place the Zoo.

One thing I didn't mention before was the cold. Most people think it is always hot in Vietnam. My first winter of 1967-68, the temp got down to two degrees Centigrade in Hanoi. We had no socks and we had no coats or sweaters. That first winter, we each had only a mosquito net and one blanket. It was a cotton blanket you could see through. I'd been cold before in my life but never like that ever, anywhere. I got so cold that my muscles tightened up completely all over my body. I couldn't relax. I was freezing all the time.

We got so cold that we would walk to keep warm. By that time, my infections were beginning to go away, and we would get up and walk at two or three o'clock in the morning, just back and forth trying to keep warm. That first winter was hard.

Sometime during the middle of the second winter (1968-69), they came in with some socks, and they eventually gave us a pullover sweatsuit type top. That helped enormously. Those first couple of winters were really something else, though.

We had a church service in our cells every Sunday. We would face the East because that was home, and we'd start with the Pledge of Allegiance. Then we'd recite the Twenty Third Psalm and then The Lord's Prayer. That was every Sunday I was in jail. My church attendance for six years was perfect, but it has never been anything like that since.

We did an enormous amount of exercise just to keep busy. That was a way to pass the time. We ran in place, we did sit ups, we did push-ups.

Guys did push-ups with their feet up against the wall, their feet high above their heads. There were records set that you wouldn't believe. There were guys doing fifteen hundred to two thousand sit-ups, developing stomach muscles that were unreal. There were guys doing four to five hundred pushups at one sitting.

Barry Bridger proceeded to set a new record when he did fifty one-armed pushups in a vertical position up against the wall, pushing all of his weight up and down with one arm. There were some physical feats that were unbelievable for people just eating rice and cabbage and pumpkin and squash, a very low-protein diet, and yet, they were able to do those things. Exercising was a great way to stay busy and keep moving to pass the time.

When we weren't exercising, we were communicating, and when we weren't doing that, there was an awful lot of time spent just lying down on a rice mat, looking up at the ceiling, thinking about happier times.

When I was in the Pigsty, I discovered an old buddy from Luke AFB in 1959. Glen Nix, one of my classmates in the F-100 course, was there in the Pigsty.

Verna, my wife at that time, thought the world of Glen. I think she had a crush on him, and that Glen had a crush on her. My first comment, when I found out he was there, was that I was damn glad he was where I could keep an eye on him. Everybody got a kick out of that. Of course, it was said in fun.

During the day, at times when it was quiet, the building sounded like it was full of woodpeckers from the tapping. The volume of communicating was amazing. Ninety nine percent of it was bullshit. But it was a great way to keep busy.

There were two meals served every day. The Vietnamese were as regular as clockwork on this. They came down and filled our water pitchers twice a day also. Occasionally, they would have fresh bread, a big loaf of what looked like French bread, but it was made out of rice, not wheat. That, of course, didn't satisfy us very much. There was rice served almost every meal. Occasionally, we got real French bread, and that was really a treat when it happened. There was a lot of pumpkin in the meals. I've eaten more pumpkin than you'll ever see in your life. I can guarantee you that.

We also were served more cabbage than the law allows and a hell of a lot of squash. There was a nearby pond that they dug weeds out of and boiled them, so we had boiled weeds as well.

Obviously, it was a vegetarian diet. I got so hungry for sweets that I would salivate thinking about a soft ice cream cone. On rare occasions, they served us sugar, just plain raw cane sugar from Cuba. They put half a cup of it on a plate, and we scarfed it down. It was amazing what that did in perking us up. It was a real shot of adrenaline. Once in a while, we got a bowl of rock salt. We needed salt badly because we sweated so much, but then it went right through us. The sugar and salt deliveries were rare events.

We were given three cigarettes a day. When I was first captured, in my first two weeks of captivity, they tried to bribe me with a cigarette. When I realized what they were doing, I quit smoking until after Tet of '68.

When Tet came around in February of that year, it was cold as I have told you. I was lonely, and I had missed Christmas and New Year's. They came and offered the best cigarettes that they had. I thought what the hell, and I started smoking again. I kept smoking after I was released and kept it up until April 7, 1983, when I quit for good.

The guys who smoked heavily bummed cigarettes from people who didn't smoke. They saved cigarette butts and re-smoked the tobacco in any kind of paper they could get their hands on. Unfortunately, Doug Burns, Dave Brose, Bobby Bagley and Don Waltman all did that, and every single one of them is dead now of lung cancer.

As a prisoner, smoking was a good way to pass time. I could kill fifteen minutes, three times a day by smoking a cigarette. I could make that damn cigarette last fifteen minutes, and that took some doing.

I brought back a package of premium North Vietnamese smokes, the best cigarettes they had. We called them Prong Songs. That' what was on the packages. They claimed that was their best. On the side in English, they had printed, "Fine Virginia tobacco." I brought back a pack of those cigarettes to show friends who smoked. I told them that we got these only twice a year, at Christmas and at Tet.

After I got out of jail, some of my old friends and I were playing bridge one night at Lichfield Park, in Arizona. I told them, "I brought something back for you."

I offered Verna a Prong Song cigarette and after a drag or two she scowled and asked, "What are you trying to do, kill me?"

I took a puff on one of them, and I couldn't believe how bad they were. In Vietnam, they had seemed pretty good.

We went into the communication business from building to building. If you look at the Zoo, you can see that the buildings are at right angles to each other. If you were in the Barn or in the Garage, the front of the buildings faced the Pool House, but you couldn't see any rooms over there because of the trees and the foliage.

So, we couldn't communicate across the camp. From the Pigsty to the Office, was an angle so you couldn't communicate there either. The only exception was one window at the far left of the Pigsty that could communicate with one window in the Stable. You can see that there is such an angle that only one room from the Pigsty could see that one room in the Stable. We became very skilled at communicating between the different buildings with a visual code. It was really an art form. We decided that we were going to require everyone to review how to communicate, once a month throughout the entire camp.

Right next to the building that we called the Kitchen, the North Vietnamese kept a pile of loose coal. They poured water in it and had some prisoners make coal balls. They used the coal balls for cooking. Next to where we made coal balls, there was a little place we called the Gate House. They kept JJ Connell there. He had been badly tortured when he was captured…and he feigned disablement from that time on.

His hands always kind of hung down off his wrists. He did such a great acting job that that the Vietnamese were convinced that they had crippled him. They gave him electrical shocks and did all kinds of things to get his system working again, but they couldn't do it. Later, JJ just sort of faded out of view and died somewhere up there. He never came home. They may have killed him to avoid the embarrassment of sending an obvious cripple home.

The guys would go over to the Gate House from the Pool House or from the Pigsty and the office. They would go to make coal balls, and JJ would tell them what was going on in the garage and in the barn. We were communicating with JJ by using a note drop.

He had managed to steal a pencil, and he gave us notes in a drop that would be hidden in a skirt around our shit buckets when we went out to empty them. We'd leave the buckets, and they'd have JJ come along, pick them up, and carry them to another point to empty them.

Anyhow, JJ made off with the buckets, extricated the note from the skirt, and put one in for us. It was dangerous as hell, but that's the way we managed to communicate. We finally had the Zoo all tied together.

Next, we had to expand communications into the Zoo annex. That was a different problem because they had a big high wall. My great friend Red McDaniel, along with Ken Fleener, an F-4 pilot, and Al Runyan, an RF-101 driver, were in the far room as you would face the Garage, the far room on the left. Charlie Southwick and I were in the far room on the right.

McDaniel and his roommates had shutters in the back of the room that the guards opened during the rest period to let in some air. The guys could walk back and forth and look out the shutters. They would see the blank wall between themselves and the Zoo annex. One day Red noticed a fluttering bit of string or thread suspended on a wire coming out of a very small hole in that wall.

He looked, and it fluttered again. He nodded, and it fluttered again. Then the string started to go in and out with the tap code. So now we could talk to the Zoo Annex.

The communications started off, "Do you see me?"

Red answered by nodding yes. We started communicating. When the shutters were open, Red would be up there, or Al, or Ken, looking out that back window. The Zoo Annex was where most of the junior officers were.

There was one room in particular at the Annex that had eight guys in it: Ed Atterberrry, John Dramisi and six others. Dramisi was absolutely going crazy, wanting to work up an escape attempt. The SRO of the Zoo was Larry Guarino, an F-105 pilot shot down in September 1964. Before Guarino came home in 1973, both of his sons were in the military. One had gone through high school, college, pilot training, and was flying combat. That's how long Guarino was a POW.

He was in the Pool House. Guarino was a major and the SRO of the whole Zoo. Now and then, somebody would get caught doing something that made the guards mad. They would be tortured and suffer horrible beatings. The Vietnamese would want to know what Guarino was saying. About once a year, the Vietnamese would play what he had told us to do or not do back to him. It was a hell of a way to live, but Larry was gutsy as hell.

He stood in there for years and years. He was one of the guys who had been SRO longer than anybody else could imagine.

Atterbury and Dramisi started to plot an escape plan. Dramisi was the driving force behind it, there is no doubt about it. I have personally interviewed the six other men who were in that room. We talked to each one of them separately in the years after we moved into the big prison after the Son Tay raid.

They all said virtually the same thing. There wasn't a single one of them who was supportive of that escape attempt. Atterberry was killed by the North Vietnamese in the ensuing torture. We think they broke his back somehow or beat him to death with a fan belt. Dramisi was just put into another world before they were finished with him.

They weren't the first to try to escape. The first two to escape were George Coker and George McKnight. Those two went out at the little prison by the power plant. It was easy, because they went out through the bars.

They left out one night and made their way down to the Red River. They got into the river and drifted down about fifteen miles. When it started to get light, they thought they had better get out and find a place to hide. The moment they were on dry land, somebody saw them and they were recaptured and brought back.

The Vietnamese beat them up pretty badly, but the two said they thought we were all going to die up there anyway. So, they just went ahead and did it.

The Vietnamese could never say they plotted and planned that escape. It was very much a spur of the moment thing. They didn't take a damned thing with them. They just went out the window and left.

The escape by Dramisi and Atterberry was a different deal. They plotted and planned for months. There was a trap door up in the ceiling of their cell, and they climbed up there. They would put a guy on a bed and lift him up, so they could get the trap door off and have access into the crawl space. The Vietnamese never went up there. A ladder had to be used. It was that high.

The two put straw hats, food and medicine up there. They stole all kinds of stuff over the months to hide there. On Saturday nights, when most of the guards were downtown drinking or whatever, the two would crawl up there and get painted up, practicing for how they intended to appear after they escaped.

I remember one of the other guys in the cell later told me how Dramisi came down one day with all of his stuff on and asked, "How do I look?"

He said, "I told him, "John, you look exactly like a five-foot eleven-inch Caucasian.""

Risner's standing order was that no escape would be made within the confines of Hanoi without outside help. That's all there was to it. By the time Dramisi and Atterberry got ready to make this escape attempt, on Saturday night, May 10, 1969, a thunderstorm came in. They thought it would cover them.

On another Saturday night earlier, they had gone up and tried to talk across the top of the building which had a double brick wall between themselves and the next cell. They were not able to communicate with Connie Trautman, the SRO that night. On yet another night, they got up in that attic, and somebody lifted Connie up from the other side. They told him what they wanted to do. They never asked Guarino for permission to escape. We found out later that it would have been turned down cold.

Connie was asked what Dramisi and Atterberry had talked about. He told them they said, "We've got to get going because the Paris peace talks are going on." That's what John Dramisi said. "The Paris peace talks are going. We've got to get out of here before they reach a peace agreement."

I am convinced beyond a shadow of a doubt, that this escape plan was all motivated by self-aggrandizement. John was really trying desperately to get in the limelight as someone who escaped from the Hanoi Hilton.

He put everybody in jeopardy. Those guys went off the roof, down the side and over a wall with all of the stuff they had stolen over the months. They were captured within two hours and brought back in just as it was getting light.

I heard the commotion, got up and looked out the window. I was in the far-right room near the Garage next to the Gatehouse. The Vietnamese brought them in the gate. The guards were yelling at them and making them run down the street separately. I saw both of them, but I didn't recognize either one of them. They were both obviously POWs running along being screamed at by the guards.

They were thrown into the Chicken Coop, which was way down at the far end. About an hour or so later, the North Vietnamese came back again. This was Sunday morning. The Vietnamese came motoring back down, hurrying, and went past where I was looking out the window. They went through that little gate at the end of the annex and burst into the room where the six remaining guys were.

The carnage was on.

Chapter 8★ The Terror

IT LASTED FOR SEVEN WEEKS. SEVEN weeks of the greatest terror that I've ever lived through in my life. They badly tortured forty-four people. They killed one guy, Ed Atterberry. They destroyed our entire communication system. There wasn't a single thing left. By the time they were through, they knew what everyone was talking about. They knew how we were communicating in every single building in every camp in the whole damn country. They broke our communications system wide open, because they tortured people to within an inch of their lives.

Through torture, the Vietnamese uncovered what we referred to as the Party Committee. Leo Thorsness was the chairman of that committee. This meant one thing in North Vietnam and something entirely different in the United States. Leo was actually the chairman of a committee to plan and organize a party after we were released to get everybody together in San Francisco.

The Vietnamese took it to mean some sort of political plot, and Leo just got the hell beat out of him. He was grievously tortured to make him tell them all about the Party Committee. It went on and on.

Red McDaniel, Ken Fleener and Al Runyan were dragged out one night, put into three separate rooms and worked over unmercifully. They tortured Red for two weeks. Two weeks with no sleep, beatings, the ropes and electrical shocks. You could hear the screams all over the camp.

Probably in the July time frame, they moved Charlie and me in with Red McDaniel and Doug Burns. The three of them were Navy guys. I was the token Air Force jock in there. I think they wanted us in with him so they could blame us when Red died.

I spent hours and hours massaging Red's hands and arms. Finally, he started to get his health back. They had beaten him almost to death. It was really close, and I thought he was going to die. I think he thought he was going to die. We worked like hell to make him as comfortable as possible.

When they moved us in with Red, he had thirty-four open wounds on him. He couldn't hear anything at all. He had blood coming out of both ears. They had broken his eardrums by beating him in the head with sandals. His arms and hands were totally useless. He couldn't wipe his ass. He couldn't eat. He couldn't light a cigarette. He could barely crawl across the room. He was an absolute vegetable. He was literally beaten within an inch of his life. I have never seen a human being tortured like that in my entire life and never want to see anything like it again.

Red was the toughest man I have ever met, mentally and physically. I have never met anyone else who could carry his jock. He is a great Christian, like Risner, and doesn't use a lot of profanity, but boy I'll tell you, he is really tough. He took what they had to hand out. He took it and took it, and they kept going after him mentally even after it was all over. He hung right in there with them. I don't know how he managed to do it.

He had brain damage. There is no question that he was badly, badly hurt. He is alive as I write this, too. Red is doing all right. He is my age, and he is a real hero of mine.

After the reign of terror, we didn't have a single way that we could communicate. They had us stopped everywhere. We had things hidden throughout the camp. The guards found every single thing. The guys coughed up their guts. They did it plainly and simply to stop the agony, because they were being killed. I mean they were hurting them so bad they couldn't stand it anymore, and they told them everything.

We told them a lot of stuff that was pure bullshit, too, but we also told them things that just absolutely wiped out everything. They came around to our room. They found out that Charlie Southwick and I were the couriers for the notes between JJ and the coal ball makers.

The officer in charge of our building would come around, open the window and look in. He had never looked in before, and he never looked in after, but during those seven weeks of terror, he looked in every day, sometimes two and three times a day as more and more information became available.

I was so damn scared, more afraid than I had ever been before in my life. I just knew they were going to come over and grab Charlie and me again, and we were going to have to cough up our guts, too. There was nothing you could do about it. You had to sit there and wait in a state of total futility. I am here to tell you, that is really a terrible feeling.

When we came home and talked about it, we realized that was the one thing for which we could never train. When schools are set up to educate people on how to prepare to handle being a prisoner, we knew we could never ever institute that kind of terror into any training. Charlie said the same thing. He had never been terrorized like that in his life before. It was excruciatingly difficult.

Then the summer was upon us, and it got really hot. We had that last room in the garage. West was to our left, and when the sun got low it blazed right on that wall. The brick got so hot that at night you couldn't comfortably put your hand on it. It was like having an iron plate sitting there heated up. We finally figured the temperature in our room had to be around 135 degrees.

It was so hot that the mosquitoes wouldn't come in. They would come up to the window, to where our window was bricked up almost to the top, and hover there. There were three or four bricks left out. That was the only ventilation that came into the room. There was almost no air movement at all at the back.

Southwick and I spent the summers of 1968, 1969, and 1970 in that room, off and on. Our arms got so red and infected from heat rash that we had two big pus balls hanging off our shoulders. At night we didn't sleep, we just fainted from the heat.

They finally gave us some fans, and it was incredible. We sat there and fanned ourselves. We woke up in the morning lying in a pool of water. The guards would come by and scream at us to put the mosquito nets up, but that was pointless because the mosquitoes wouldn't come into our room. It was too hot for them. It was unbelievable to have lived through that. I think back on that, and I don't know how in the hell I did it. But there was no place else to go. I mean you couldn't run. I'll never forgive them for that.

That escape attempt was disastrous for us. It gained us absolutely nothing. We didn't even get respect out of it, because the guys didn't make it. All the Vietnamese did was pay a lot more attention to us. It took us months and months to get back any kind of communications. It was terrifying to communicate with your next-door neighbor, because the guards were right on top of you. The terror went on for the rest of the year until September of 1969, when Ho Chi Minh died.

Chapter 9★ The Death of Uncle Ho

WE KNEW THAT HE HAD DIED. I woke up at 4:00 or 4:30 in the morning. They were playing the Ho Chi Minh song. It went on and on, over and over. One of the guys asked, "Why are they playing that song?"

I replied, "I'll tell you why. Ho just died. The name of the game now is to keep our heads down." I passed that on to the SRO in the building. At the time, we were back in the Pigsty again.

The message was, "Don't show any signs of exuberance about Ho's death, because that might get the terror going again." The guys saw the light, and we kept our mouths shut.

In another few days, they announced the date for his funeral. They played some music over the camp radio and talked a little bit about him. All I did was sit there and think, "Well, the old sonofabitch is dead."

At the same time, the news wasn't that good. Of the five men who ran that country, Ho was preeminent in his knowledge of the West. None of the rest of them had Ho's savvy about what was going on. About a month after Ho Chi Minh's death, the Russians and Chinese came. Things started to happen. Our lives started to change dramatically. For the North Vietnamese, it was almost unbelievable speed, because generally, they were glacially slow to react.

One day they would come along and close the blinds, the wooden blinds, when it was nap time. Then they would come back around and pull them open again. That helped us, because then we would be up in the window, looking out through the slats to see any feet approaching. We could communicate without getting caught.

One day, Charlie Southwick got up there and was peeking out to see any guards. I was communicating. When I finished and stepped away from the wall, I said, "I'm clear."

Charlie stepped down off the windowsill and then reached up to push open the blinds. When he pushed, it hit one of the guards who had been standing out there. Charlie hadn't seen him.

The guard let out a scream and ran off to get the officer who looked over the building. Pretty soon he came and opened the door. Of course, we all stood up and bowed. He looked in the peephole, and he started to say, "You will be..." and the next thing he would have said was, " ... punished," but he stopped. He got sort of a contrite look on his face, slammed the little window shut, and off he went.

I said, "Charlie, I'm probably grasping at straws, but I think something has happened. I don't think we're going to see him again." In fact, the guy never, ever came back.

Shortly thereafter, they started to take the bricks out of the windows, and a breeze would come through at night. It was a whole different thing. The food improved a little bit but not a hell of a lot.

All the heavy torture stopped after Ho died.

NGÀY VIẾT (Dated) 24 November 1970

Dear Parents, I was delighted to receive your letter and that you are back in Corvallis in your old home. As you reach the end of your active school careers I want you to know how proud of both of you I am. Your contribution to education has been outstanding. I pray this Christmas will be a happy one and that the new year sees us together again. Love to my Parents-In-Law

Love Jack

GHI CHÚ (N.B.):

1. Phải viết rõ và chỉ được viết trên những dòng kẻ sẵn *(Write legibly and only on the lines)*.
2. Gia đình gửi đến cũng phải theo đúng mẫu, khuôn khổ và quy định này *(Notes from families should also conform to this proforma)*.

Chapter 10★ Memories from my Childhood

THE DAYS AND WEEKS AND MONTHS of captivity blended into an eternity of pain, fear, and boredom. When I was not under threat of immediate duress and had time to do so, and over the years there was plenty of that, I reflected back on things from the past as everyone did.

I was born in Eugene, Oregon, on 16 December 1931. My parents started me off in the first grade when I was five years old. It was legal then. I wish they had waited until I was six because it came back to plague me years later. People thought I had maturity I really didn't. That extra year would have helped me a lot.

I went to three different elementary schools, two years each. My parents moved from home to home. They kept working on improving their lot. They were both public school teachers or administrators. My dad left over a quarter of a million dollars of assets that they had built up. They accomplished that by buying and working on homes and selling them for a profit.

We eventually ended up living in a really nice home in Eugene. I became the catcher of the softball team when I was in the third grade, and I caught for that team for four years.

During the early days of World War II, my mother became the director of the Eugene vocational school where she trained B-17 mechanics. Two influential people came to visit us during the early course of the war. Eleanor Roosevelt came to Eugene and went through the vocational school. She was clearly the eyes and ears of the President. Hap Arnold also came to Eugene on a trip supposedly to inspect how my mom was doing training B-17 mechanics. His real reason for being there was to go fishing on the McKinsey River, and my dad took him up there.

At dinner, the night before they went up there, General Arnold sat at the table which was illuminated by candlelight. He had on his full uniform, four stars and all. I was really impressed.

My brother and I were kept in the kitchen with the housekeeper. Finally, we were invited in to meet General Arnold.

He looked at me and asked, "Jackie, what do you want to be when you grow up?"

By this time, I was twelve years old. I said, "I want to be a pilot, sir."

"Oh really? Good. What kind of a pilot do you want to be?"

I thought that he was a bomber pilot. I said, "I want to be a fighter pilot."

He laughed.

My father was the second son of Jed and Sarah Van Loan, and my grandfather was a dirt farmer who had come out from Minnesota. My dad was born in 1901, while his parents were in route to Monmouth in a place called Hood River, Oregon.

My grandfather had a sixty-five-acre farm, and that's where he lived and worked until he died at age 96. The day he died, he was visiting my mother and father in Corvallis which was about twenty miles from Monmouth. He said to my mother that morning, "I have to get home to till the corn."

She told him, "You can do that tomorrow. There's no great rush."

He said, "No, I have to get home today," and he was so insistent about it that she put him on the bus. My grandfather always called the bus "the stage."

My mother phoned my uncle Hugh who met my grandfather at the bus station and took him out to his farm. The old man changed into his bib overalls, and Hugh left, telling him he'd be back after a while. He found grandfather by the last row of corn. He'd tilled the last row of corn and then dropped dead. He died with his boots on.

He was clearly my most unforgettable character. My grandfather was very conservative, and he listened to the Richfield Reporter. He tolerated me as long as I was seen and not heard. Even though I was his first grandson, he was not really interested in me getting in the way.

I had some grandfather stories that I would relate. I told them while I was in jail. Stories that were told well would get around the system up there in Hanoi. My grandfather stories became something in demand, so when I moved into a new room, guys would say, "Hey, tell us about your grandfather."

My grandfather had three sons. The oldest was my Uncle Berchard. Wendell, my dad, came second, and Hugh was the third son. The old man raised those three boys on that farm. My Uncle Berchard became a renowned, world class gynecologist, a diplomat. In medical terms, that means he was top of the line.

My dad earned a PHD and became president of the first community college in Oregon. Hugh was the postmaster in Monmouth. So, they all did well. They grew up in the little farmhouse, in essence a one bedroom with a loft. It had no indoor plumbing until the 30s when a bathroom was added. We also got electricity at about the same time.

One day, I was out playing with our dog, a German Sheppard. I was throwing a stick to the dog. Then I started to tease him by gesturing like I was throwing the stick and then putting it under my arm when my dad walked by. We were all down there to help harvest.

Anyway, I was teasing this dog, and my dad walked by and said, "Either play with the dog or don't play with him, don't tease him."

I didn't stop. I was holding the stick up with my left hand, and the dog jumped for the stick. He missed it and came down on my thumb. I have the scar to this day. He about bit my thumb right off. I screamed, and the dog yelped. He didn't mean to bite me.

I went up to the farmhouse and into the kitchen. My grandmother grabbed a towel. She put it on my hand and applied pressure on it. She then told my mother to start the car. My grandfather came in. He said, what happened. She said, your dog bit Jackie. My grandfather reached up over the transom and got down his shotgun as my dad walked into the room.

He said, "Where you going with that gun?"

Grandfather said, "I'm going to shoot that damn dog."

My dad roared at him, "Don't shoot the dog, shoot the boy. It's the boy's fault." And my grandfather turned and stared at me with a speculative look. It scared the hell out of me, and I never ever teased another animal again.

STEVEN'S CHRISTENING (JACK WITH STEVEN, HIS GRANDFATHER AND HIS FATHER)

When my first son was christened in 1960 or thereabouts, my grandfather came down from Monmouth for the christening. He outlived my grandmother by twenty some odd years. He was a few years older than she was when they were married. She died in her early 70s, and he lived until 96. He came down for Steven's christening. One of the great pictures I have of my life is of four generations of Van Loans on the day he was christened, my grandfather, my father, me, and Steven.

When my grandfather got off the bus, my dad picked him up. The old man was 92 years old at that time. My dad noticed that his suit was a little bit tattered. He had had it for over 40 years. He said to my grandfather, I'm going to take you to my tailor and have a new suit made for you. My grandfather said, thank you, and my dad had him fitted for a new suit. Later when he came down for church, he was wearing his old suit of clothes.

My dad looked at him and asked, "Don't you like your new suit?"

"Yes, it's great."

"Why don't you have it on?"

"I'm saving it."

"What for?"

"Eastern Star and Grange."

My dad said, "You damned old fool, get back up there and put on your new suit before we're late for church."

He came down to see my dad one time and had a coffee can under his arm. He said, "This is all the money I have in the world, and I want you to have it." He got out the bills. It added up to about $2500. My dad was stunned. He thought grandfather might have robbed a bank or something. That was in the early 1950s, and the money was what he had saved. A big cash year on that farm was $500. They traded for everything. They didn't have any cash. The only actual money came from the milk and eggs that they sold.

He said, "I want you to have it."

My father said, "What about Berchard?"

"He isn't getting anything. He doesn't need anything. Hugh can use the farm, and it's the most valuable thing I have."

My dad took it and invested it in savings and loan stock in my grandfather's name and his name jointly. The investment went up and split thirteen to one and did that twice. So, my grandfather's money accrued to about $75,000.

My grandfather never drove. He walked everywhere, but he had a team of huge Percheron horses that he got in his seventies. These horses were about two years old, and they were barely broken to any kind of harness. The old man couldn't put the harnesses on the horses in the barn. He had to take them out by a hayrack. There was a wagon there. He'd get up on the wagon and put the harnesses on. The horses were just too damn big for him.

One day, he was behind the horses, cleaning the crap out through the window, and a little dog trotted by. One of the horses kicked at the dog and missed. The horse hit my grandfather right in the chest and literally blew him through the hole he's throwing the crap out. His chest was virtually crushed. He crawled up to the house, really hurt. He gets that gun to go down and shoot the horse. My uncle Hugh happened by and took the gun away from him.

Later, my grandfather recovered and was plowing with these horses. They were so big and powerful that they could pull a sit-down plow that he could sit on. Most plows were one 14-inch bottom plow. He had two twelve-inch bottom plows on this one rig, and he could walk behind it or sit on it.

Those horses were so strong they could pull him all day long. If anything happened and the horses got spooked and started to run, he'd just drop the plow in the ground and that would stop them.

On one occasion, he was plowing down by the turn in the field, and some birds flew by. The birds startled the horses and they took off. He dropped both plows into the ground, but these horses kept right on going. They broke a four-by-four singletree that they were harnessed to out in front, and it threw my grandfather out in front of the plow which came up and hit him in the head. It all but scalped him. The horses kept on going, destroying this plow until they ran into a fence. It damned near killed my grandfather.

He staggered back up to the house with blood all over him. He was going to kill both horses this time. My Uncle Hugh was there and said, "No, you're going to sell them."

He did. Then my grandfather bought a Ford tractor. He bought it when he was in his seventies and drove it for twenty years. He would even drive it into town. It was very slow.

My grandfather walked everywhere, and finally my Uncle Berchard, a doctor, said he was getting too old to walk which is the most foolish thing I've ever heard. My uncle said he needed to have a car. My grandfather had never driven one.

My uncle got an old Pontiac for him that had the old-type upholstery in it. He never learned to properly shift it. So, he would put it in reverse, floor it, and pop the clutch. It would come out of that garage like a jackrabbit. People used to really watch out when they went by his house because that car might come screaming out. Then he would jam the thing into high gear, because he couldn't shift gears, and it would leap forward. It was thrilling to ride with him.

He seldom drove it, but one Thanksgiving my aunt asked my grandfather to take me and go downtown to get some bread. When he came to the stop light, the only one in Monmouth, he eased through it, because if he stopped, he couldn't get it started again. Unfortunately, he didn't see a guy standing by the road and he hit him with the left front fender. Grandfather pulled back on the steering wheel and hollered, "Whoa!"

Grandfather was sitting there, shaking like a leaf. The guy gets up and dusts himself off. He wasn't hurt. It was the town sheriff.

He had just flattened the sheriff, who looked in the car and said, "Where are you going, Jed?"

"Bread."

"Jacky, get in the back," the sheriff instructed me.

He drove us down to the baker. He told grandfather to get the bread, which he did. Then he drove us home, put the car in the garage, took the keys and told Uncle Hugh, "Take this car back to Portland. He isn't driving a car again."

The Depression made a tremendous impression on my parents and grandparents. They literally put money in cans buried in the back yard, because they didn't trust the banks. My grandfather didn't have a driver's license. He couldn't pass the test. Back then, people didn't get excited about things like that.

I came home from Warren AB in 1955, and my mother said, "I'm glad you're home. Your grandfather is really mad at us and won't let us back in the house."

"What did you do?" I asked.

"Well, we threw out some old newspapers."

"Did you ask permission?"

"No, they were just cluttering up the loft for thirty or forty years. I threw them out. It was a mess." My mother said, "We're painting the house, and I want you to go with us."

We went back down to Corvallis. Grandfather had a gravel driveway He could hear a car coming but couldn't see well.

I got out. He wasn't carrying a gun, but it was like he had a gun in his hand. "Jackie, is that you?"

"Yes, glad to see you."

"Do you know what these people have done?"

"They threw out your newspapers. They were wrong, but you can go down to the library. They have every copy on tape. They can expand the print, and you can see it." That seemed to appease him.

My grandfather lived to be ninety-six. He ate well, walked everywhere, and he never smoked or drank. However, my dad said later that grandfather would turn to him occasionally, and say, "Wendell, fetch me some of that stuff that makes me feel good." Dad would mix up some screwdrivers, and grandfather would drink one or two.

My Uncle Charlie served in the Second World War. He was in the Seabees, and he was a very tough man. He hated the American Red Cross, because they had shown up at a beach somewhere and charged him a quarter for coffee and donuts. He never forgot that. He said, "If I ever hear of anyone in my family contributing to the American Red Cross, I'll disown them forever." I never forgot that.

Oregon really was a conservative state then and a marvelous place to grow up. I went to Parkrose High School in Portland, Oregon. Dad was the assistant superintendent of schools at a place called Vanport, Van for Vancouver, Port for Portland on the Oregon side. They housed thirty-five thousand of Henry Kaiser's shipyard workers there during the war.

Franklin Roosevelt died while I lived there, and it scared the hell out of me. I was thirteen or fourteen, and I thought he was my protector. It wasn't until years later I found out how much real harm he had done with some of the socialistic programs he had initiated. Ed Wells is one of my closest friends, and all I have to do is to mention Roosevelt to him, and it ruins the rest of his day.

Roosevelt was very unpopular in Oregon during the depression. The Oregonian business community was absolutely opposed to his programs, the socialism that he brought into the government started in the early 30s when he said, "All we have to fear is fear itself."

That was the situation in which I grew up. Then during my senior year in high school, my dad got the job as superintendent of schools in Corvallis, so we moved there in 1946. My mom and dad had done something that I thought was the bravest thing I could imagine.

At the height of the depression, in the middle thirties, when I was five or six years old, my dad took a sabbatical from Roosevelt Junior High school where he was the principal. He went to Stanford University to get his PHD. He had a master's from the University of Oregon, and he believed to get a doctorate from Oregon wouldn't help him that much.

He and my mother had decided that he had to get a PHD from Stanford. He left my mother and three kids and off he went. It was really a gutsy decision, and one I have always respected. Afterward, he built eighty-five million dollars' worth of school buildings by floating bonds. Eventually both my parents became PHDs.

In high school, I liked and played sports. I was a pretty good football player and played center on the varsity team. In baseball, I was better. I made All State. However, I did a crappy job of doing schoolwork. I am embarrassed at how bad I was. Had it not been for the fact that excellent dinner-table-English was spoken in our home all the time, I never would have passed an English course.

I received a good education at home. I went to Oregon State and was on probation for three straight terms. I liked to party, and I knew I was in danger of being drafted and sent to the Korean war.

About halfway through my sophomore year, Earl Goddard, the Dean of the school of business, saw me out in the hall and asked if I had a minute? I said, "Yes, sir."

He said, "You know, you're an embarrassment, to Oregon State, to your family, to everyone I know. What the hell is wrong with you? You are scheduled to take a class from me, and if you don't pay attention to what's going on, I'm going to flunk your ass." He really chewed my butt. No one had ever chewed on me like that. I went to work, halfway through my sophomore year, and I made the Dean's List at the end of that year.

I graduated from Oregon State University in 1954, after five years.

Chapter 11 ★ Loosening the Chains

HO CHI MINH DIED ON THE 6th of September 1969. After a couple weeks of the guards moping around and his funeral, they started with almost incredible speed to make our lives better.

The windows had been bricked up to within a couple or three brick widths of the top of all the windows. The North Vietnamese proceeded to not only knock out those bricks all the way down to the windowsill, but they also removed the walls between the rooms on either side. So instead of having eight rooms in buildings such as the Pigsty, we now had four rooms. Instead of having three or four men to one room, we now had five to seven.

This made things immeasurably better. We had more room, and the breeze would come through at night. Before, when the guards had opened the door at night to yell at us to put up mosquito nets, we often sensed that the air outside was twenty to thirty degrees cooler than in the room. Sure enough, that was correct.

The night air was now actually rather pleasant. Instead of being sopping wet in the morning from sweat, we had only a small pool of sweat, if any. It was a dramatic improvement to be able to sleep comfortably. Also, we could see the guys when they were walking by the windows.

The guards still made a big deal out of us not talking to each other, but they weren't around as much to check on whether we were tapping on the walls. It must have been obvious to the guards that there were many eyes watching them. We felt a lot more comfortable tapping on the walls.

They just kind of backed away from all the atrocious treatment. Months earlier, during the period of time in jail that we called the purge of 1969, they had brutally tortured forty-four people. They tortured Ed Atterberry to death. Then, for the most part after Ho's death, the vicious torturing ceased.

Some guards came in one day. They jerked open the door and gave me the little chopping motion of one hand on the other wrist. That meant to put on my long, dark red jacket and faded red pajamas we wore. That was our formal dress, so to speak. That also meant that I was getting suited up to go on over and see an officer.

I can't tell you how those seven weeks of terror had worn on me. I mean, it was really difficult for Charlie Southwick and myself. His name by the way was Charles Everett Southwick. Most people call him Ev Southwick. I call him Charlie. He was clearly the element of balance that kept me from going right over the edge. He was a tremendous source of power in our room and always a terrific guy.

Charlie was a graduate of the University of Washington, went through a ROTC program there, then into the Navy. He flew the F-8 and later the F-4. When he got out of prison, he went to Hastings Law School and was a political lobbyist for many years. He now lives in San Diego. He was one of the best friends I ever had in my life. I tried to be a source of comfort to him also in those seven weeks of terror, but I'll tell you it was really hard.

The guard brought me in to see Spot, the building officer. He had spots on his face, white, albino-like spots and that's what we called him. I sat down opposite Spot, and he looked at me.

Spot asked me how the food was. How this was this and how was that? It was all bullshit. Then he said, suddenly, "Who is the SRO in your building?"

I said, "I don't know what you're talking about."

He just looked at me and smiled.

They had broken us so badly he knew I was scared half to death. Suddenly the door opened. There in the doorway, leaning up against the transom was WTG. That stood for the World's Tallest Gook. This guy was an enlisted guy, and he was standing there and holding a fan belt in his right hand. He was twitching it back and forth like he had a snake in his hand.

I have to say this. After all that they had done to us, it was terrifying. There was the WTG. I thought well, he's going to start beating on me again, and I won't last very damn long, because the method was just unbelievable. You would have your pants pulled down and then they made you lie on your stomach. Then a couple of those assholes would come at you with those fan belts, one on either side of you, with your bare ass hanging out there. They would lash you as hard and fast as they could swing those fan belts…and down it all would come on your ass.

They hit Jim Kasler with those things two hundred times … and he still carries the marks of it. I mean the scars on Jim's back and buttocks are unbelievable. They hit me four or five times, and I was done for the day. It was incredible agony and brutal torture.

WTG stood there flicking that whip back and forth as if to say, "You make a wrong move here, and I'm going after you." They didn't have to convince me of that. I knew it.

Anyhow, we were all relieved that now things were obviously getting better. The guys were saying that the reason for that was because Ho had died. I tried to tell them, that wasn't the reason at all. I guarantee you that was not the reason.

The reason things were getting better was that they had someone to blame now. They could blame Ho Chi Minh. I believed that one day, we would eventually find out that the Russians or the Chinese or both of them had something to say about it.

At that time, I still had not received any mail. I was there two and one-half years before they gave me a piece of mail. Then I was given the opportunity to write a letter. We started to get some playing cards so we could play a little bridge without having to make up cards from toilet paper.

We could also play Gin Rummy. I went to Vietnam thinking I was a good Gin Rummy player. I'd played a good bit of Gin at the Wigwam Country Club in Lichfield Park, Arizona, against some pretty tough guys. I also thought I was a pretty good Hollywood gin player. Then I got to Hanoi and discovered I was a rank amateur. I wasn't any competition at all for guys like Red McDaniel and Dwight Sullivan. I really went to work on it and actually became a very good gin rummy player. Eventually, I could beat those guys.

Then when we got up on the China border, I moved in with Kyle “Red” Berg and found I was no match for him. We played all the time, and I finally got to the point where I could finally beat Kyle about two games out of ten.

I told him that we were going to go back to Lichfield, the two of us would play partners, and we’d make a million dollars. This guy was really great. We never did that though. We just had a lot of fun playing together.

Chapter 12★ Delegations

WE STARTED TO GET DELEGATIONS of anti-Americans coming to Hanoi. Some who made two or three trips, were Dave Dillinger, Cora Weiss, Pete Seeger, and Jane Fonda, of course, came up there with Tom Hayden.

Fonda was the most public and famous. I have a picture of her sitting in the gunner's chair of a 37-millimeter anti-aircraft gun with a North Vietnamese helmet on, playing at shooting down one of our airplanes.

She came to Hanoi, talked to the press, and went on Hanoi radio, beseeching our soldiers in the South to lay down their arms She went out and posed with our enemy, making propaganda photo ops for the North Vietnamese.

In my mind, she is clearly guilty of treason. I read where she was given some sort of award as one of the top 100 women of this country. In fact, she is one of the top traitors of all time. She and Tokyo Rose are in exactly the same status, as far as I am concerned. Tom Hayden is some California political hack posted out there in Santa Monica as I write this.

He and his wife came to Hanoi and spoke on the radio. We had to sit there and listen to those two damned communist bastards talk. I still get upset thinking about them. I have never made a speech yet without mentioning how we felt about Hanoi Jane Fonda and Tom Hayden, and I have spoken hundreds of times of our experience in North Vietnam.

The thing that is important to remember about all of those "peace loving" visitors to Hanoi is that they didn't come there to protest the war. They used Hanoi as a platform for their anti-American agendas, not anti-war views. They didn't mind the war at all as long as America didn't win. We have all of this as a matter of record on Hanoi Radio.

After the guards became less pugnacious, and the officers less vindictive toward us, there were guys there who suddenly grew a pair. Some people who had been notably submissive for months and years suddenly became aggressive toward the guards once the torture stopped.

I tried to be even-handed with the Vietnamese. Charlie Southwick set the example very well in our room for years and years. Trying to be a tough guy with them was a waste of time. You would get the hell kicked out of you. On the other hand, you couldn't just cave into them either. No matter how bad you were scared, you had to keep up some kind of a front.

But now that the real pressure was off, a few guys who had been somewhat cowering, some to the point of boot licking, started to show aggressiveness toward the Vietnamese. Some of the leadership had to step in and tell them to calm down, because they might trigger reprisals and cause the Vietnamese to resume their torture. That was bothersome to watch. There were only a very few of our guys who did this. They got counseled by some of our seniors, and that behavior stopped.

They added to the guards as the number of prisoners grew. They hardly ever changed out a guard once he was working with us. The only time that they ever really changed guards was after the escape purge. Under torture, they found out that there had been a couple of women who worked in there carrying water around on poles who would stand around outside. We had seen them out there with little pocket mirrors, putting on makeup, sort of getting themselves dolled up, combing their hair before they started passing out water and trying to impress us.

That got back to the people who were doing the torturing, and those women disappeared. One of them somehow ended up in an ambulance with Fred Cherry going to the army hospital to have his stomach X-rayed.

Anyway, a woman came in the room where Fred Cherry was. He was downtown in the hospital, and he swears and be damned that this woman came into the hospital room where he was in a bed. She climbed up on top of him and began sort of humping him a little bit.

Whether it happened or not, I don't know, but Fred has a least a thousand jokes, all of them were bad. He is a marvelous American and a terrific guy. He was an Instructor Pilot at Luke for years and was one of my IPs. I was damn lucky to have him.

The North Vietnamese tried as hard as they could to get Fred to cross over to the "people's" side. They tried to get him to speak out against the United States and the way the U.S. treated blacks. He would not play that game. When they finally realized that Fred was not going to cross over, it became brutal for him. They just couldn't understand why Fred wouldn't abandon his position.

What they did not understand was that Fred was first of all, an American, number two, a fighter pilot, and number three, he was a black guy, in that order. He was an American first, last, and always.

When they discovered that Fred wasn't going to quit, and he wasn't going home early out of turn, things got very bad for him. They beat him so savagely they broke his ribs. Then they tied him up and cut off all his circulation. They threw him into the building I was in. I'll never forget it. He was all stove up, broken ribs, couldn't use his hands, yet he was banging out communications to us with his head. Fred Cherry's one of the toughest men I ever met. I would follow him to hell and back and never think twice about it.

Norm McDaniel was a navigator. Great voice, a very quiet guy. Just did his job, did a terrific job over the years and never quit. They tried to get him to cave in, too, but they didn't work him over quite as hard as they did with Fred. I guess because Norm was shot down a year or two later than Fred was.

Fred was shot down by his own airplane. The F-105 had a bad characteristic while firing the Gatling gun. It could build up gas pressure inside the gun bay. Once in a great while, the damned gun bay door would get blown off from the pressure, and it could be drawn into the engine intake. That's what happened to Freddy. He didn't get hit by anything. His engine ate his own gun bay door, and he had to step over the side. That got him captured. It must have been a hell of a way to spend seven and a half years, thinking about some engineer's design problem wiping you out.

We had more interrogations, or as we called the "quizzes" after that, but the Vietnamese had reduced the pressure. That also took pressure off themselves, so things began to become boring.

We weren't in a fight with them as much as we had been before, and things were more relaxed. We were communicating all the time. They knew what we were doing, but by then, it was no big deal. We weren't causing any kind of riots either, because we were communicating. They knew what our command structure was, and they weren't asking us about it. Things went along like that for a time.

Chapter 13★ Traitors and Heroes

DOWN AT ONE END OF THE CAMP in the Pigsty at the far end of the building, the Vietnamese held two guys named Edison Miller and Eugene Wilber. Gene Wilber is a retired Navy captain now and Ed Miller is a retired Marine Corps lieutenant colonel. In my personal opinion, both of them committed treason while we were in jail.

Both of them had their command privileges taken away from them. Both of them sued many members of NAM-POW after we came back, but the case was eventually thrown out of court. They sued for defamation of character, but truth is a defense, and nothing ever came of it.

In my opinion, both of those guys violated our code. I believe both of them acted against direct orders. Both of them collaborated, actively and openly, with the North Vietnamese. Both of them turned in their fellow prisoners for communicating. Both of them told the North Vietnamese about how when we wrote letters to the United States, we altered the letters to get secret messages out. They betrayed us by tipping the North Vietnamese off to that. They were clearly guilty of offenses that warranted their being subjected to courts martial.

Norris Overly was one of twelve men who came home early against orders. The only one who came home early under orders was the seaman, Doug Hegdahl. Doug had fallen off the USS Canberra one night when the guns fired, and the shock blew him overboard. He floated around there all night long. Finally, he was picked up by a Vietnamese fishing boat.

The North Vietnamese were convinced at first that he was a CIA agent, and they hammered the hell out of him. They finally decided he wasn't an agent, but that he was just stupid. In fact, he was neither a CIA agent, nor was he stupid. He was a young, eighteen-year-old kid. When they let Hegdahl go, we knew that it would be tantamount to turning loose the world press, if in fact, he got the audience we hoped he would get at home. There is no doubt in my mind that when Dick Stratton told him to do something, Doug was going to do exactly what he was told.

I was delighted that Doug was ordered to step across the line a little bit to get the Vietnamese to let him go, but he didn't have to do very much, because they wanted to get rid of him. They didn't know what the hell to do with him. He was a Boy Scout kid up there amongst all of us old guys, and he was of no use to them whatsoever. He fooled them, and they thought that he was not very bright. That was a mistake on their part, and that worked out very well. Hegdahl had a photographic memory and he memorized the names of every known POW held at that time.

He lived with Stratton for a good bit of time, and Stratton gave him a direct order to go home early if he possibly could. He gave Doug a tremendous amount of information, and Doug memorized it. He has it memorized to this day. He can spout off about 375 names without hesitation.

Later, one of the seniors, Ted Guy, came in there. He didn't think it was an appropriate order initially, and he countermanded it. Then Stratton talked to him more persuasively and told him that we were losing people. If we could get one young man released with all this information, it would be useful. Guy eventually agreed.

The North Vietnamese released Doug in August of 1969, In September of 1969, Ho Chi Minh died. Stratton had instructed Hegdahl very strongly that he was only to debrief the Secretary of Defense, Melvin Laird.

Hegdahl eventually did debrief Laird. He gave him about a two and one-half hour briefing without stopping. Laird then told Nixon, and that information ended up on the front pages of American newspapers. That is the first time our plight had ever been publicized like that. The Chinese, the Russians, the whole world knew all about it.

This happened at a time when both the Soviet premier Alexei Kosygin, and Chinese leader, Chou en Lai, came to Hanoi to pay their respect to Ho. While the Soviets and the Chinese were never seen publicly together in those days, we know that they both told the North Vietnamese to ease up and to stop embarrassing the Communist cause with the heavy-handed treatment of the prisoners if they wanted continued support.

From that time on, the serious torture stopped. We were still slapped around and beaten but nothing like before. They were able to blame that on Ho Chi Minh. I believe it was actually Giap's fault, the defense minister. He was responsible. Ho knew the value that Americans placed on our prisoners.

As the pressure on us lessened, we became aware of Robbie Risner's directives. He said that no one would accept amnesty. No one would go home early. We were all to go home in turn. No one was to read on the radio. No one was to see foreign delegations.

No one was to attempt escape without outside help. If you went out in the street, you would be captured right away because you would look like a six-foot white Caucasian and stand out like a sore thumb.

Norris Overly was in the first group of three that came out of the Plantation and went home early.

Those who left early were told by our captors that they had to write a letter of apology to the North Vietnamese people. They had to ask Ho Chi Minh for amnesty, and they had to beg forgiveness.

They did that, and they were released. That, of course, was a real shot in the ass for all of us who remained, because they had done exactly what they were told not to do.

Wes Rumble, was another who went home early.

I was asked when I got back, "Did you tell Rumble that he was not to accept amnesty, that he was not to go home out of turn?"

I said, "I told him that."

"Did he understand?"

I answered, "How the hell would I know if he understood? I was passing information under very difficult circumstances."

When Everett Alvarez was first captured in August of 1964, the Vietnamese didn't really know what to do with him. He was up there all by himself. They were bringing him in catered food from restaurants and Red Cross packages. He was there for about nine months before Heyden Lockhart, the second man was shot down.

They brought a Frenchman in to talk to Alvie, and he said, "I know Ho, and all you have to do is to say you are sorry you came up here, and I'll tell Ho. He will release you then." Alvie knew that didn't sound right, and he didn't do it. He stayed there for about nine years. Common sense told you that accepting an early release wasn't the thing to do.

They released Wes Rumble early.

A few years after my return, I was appointed as the Deputy for Operations, the 9th Air Force. At my very first staff meeting, I had seven full colonels who were department heads, and I had asked them to be there. I had been a wing commander, and my boss, General Braswell, had moved me up to be the DO of 9th Air Force. There sat a young major, whom I didn't recognize at all. I had seen a picture of Rumble, but I didn't know him.

I said, "Major, what's your name?"

He answered, "Sir, I'm Wes Rumble."

I said, "Wes Rumble?" I could see him sort of sinking down in his chair. "Were you in Hanoi?"

He said, "Yes, sir."

I then stood up and stated, "Gentlemen, this briefing is disbanded. You all are dismissed." Then I got up and walked up to the Chief of Staff's office and said, "You have a choice. You can tell General Braswell to get this guy out of here, or I will. I'm going home. If he wants me to be the DO of 9th Air Force, I am looking forward to working with him, but I will not stay here with Wes Rumble in the unit."

I was called at home a few minutes after I arrived and told that Rumble was reassigned, and that I would never see him again. I didn't.

There were twelve guys who came home early. As I mentioned, one of them was Doug Hegdahl. He is a member of the NAMPOW, and he is welcome at our affairs. The other eleven are not and are barred from ever being members. I will never be around any of them in any shape or form.

Some guys got bad press back home but didn't deserve it. Dick Stratton had been on the cover of Life Magazine with his bowing act. The press portrayed us as Pavlov's dogs. Stratton continued to piss off the Vietnamese after that. One day they had him out for a quiz, and he said something that irritated them, so they put him alone in a room that had absolutely no light at all. It was completely black, and he was there for about six weeks.

I was in the room next door, and it was very difficult to communicate with him, because I was alone, too. There was a small window in my door with a slide to block it. The guards could quietly open it, but I couldn't hear it. I had to be careful, because I knew if I was caught communicating with Stratton, I would be beaten. Finally, Jim Bailey, a new man was put in with me. He would stand in front of the door, blocking the view, and I could regularly communicate with Stratton.

I could get my cup, hold my nose so my voice was contained and projected forward in that cup, and I could talk right through the wall. I passed a lot of information to Stratton about how his appearance with that Pavlov dog routine had been received in the American press, and the uproar it had caused. That is really what pissed off the North Vietnamese. They were accused of brainwashing, and Stratton brought it all on with his quick wit.

The Secretary of the Navy elected not to court martial any of those who came home early. In my opinion, that was a gross error. They clearly should have been tried by court martial, because we had the goods on them coming and going. However, the war was unpopular, and the government leaders didn't have the guts to prosecute these traitors. In previous wars, they would have been put in front of a firing squad.

I suppose the government chose not to because they didn't want to have them come back and say, well what about Stockdale, how about Risner, and Denton, guys who talked on the camp radio as they did, guys who went to see delegations. In fact, when Denton went to a delegation, he flashed out "torture" by blinking his eyes in Morse Code, sending a message that was seen all over the world.

The difference was that when Stockdale, Risner, Denton or any of them went out of the Hanoi Hilton to see a delegation, they had been severely tortured to do it, and they had the scars to prove it.

Miller and Wilbur did not get tortured at all. They did their treasonous acts willingly. They were trying to get an early release. They collaborated desperately in attempt to follow the path of Jim Lowe, Wes Rumble, and Norris Overly. They tried to curry favor with the North Vietnamese to let them go home early.

In the final analysis, what the North Vietnamese did was almost laughable. These were two guys who were in perfect condition. They were not injured at all. They put them in with the first group to be released when we all were. That is how much earlier they got to go home. By rank of shoot down date, they should have been going out in the second or third group. The North Vietnamese put them in with the first group, which meant they put them in with Stockdale, Risner, Denton and all of those old guys.

Robbie Risner was the Vice Commander of the 4th Allied POW Wing. The commander was John Flynn. Flynn later became the Inspector General of the Air Force, and has since passed away. Risner was a tremendous guy. On the way out, Risner gave Miller and Wilbur a direct order. They were not to say anything to anybody without clearing it with him. They were to say nothing to the press, nothing to anyone. He told them, if you don't think I can't make this order stick, just try me. They said nothing.

After we came home, we went to the White House POW dinner in April of 1973. There were thirty-five hundred people in the big tents set up for us. We were all transported there in busses. My then wife, Verna and I went together and walked to our table a bit early. I told Verna, "You need to check and see who the head of the table is, who our host is." It turned out to be Admiral Zumwalt.

We were standing behind our chairs when, on the other side of the table, a very handsome Navy captain walked up in uniform, full mess dress with a very attractive woman I presumed to be a wife. I stuck my hand out, kind of leaning across the table and I said, "Captain, I'm Jack Van Loan."

He replied, "Oh, yeah, Jack. I'm Gene Wilbur."

I jerked my hand back, "You son of a bitch. What in the hell are you doing here?"

He recoiled. I literally started going across the table after him.

Verna reached out and grabbed my belt and snapped, "Not here, for God's sake."

I mean I was in a rage, instantly. It was incomprehensible to me that he would have the damned guts to show up at dinner with us after committing treason and betraying us in prison. It was unbelievable.

I thought, we have really got our hands full here. I wondered who the SRO was here at this table. It wasn't going to be Wilbur, because he had his ability to command taken away from him.

I moved around the table, and Wilbur started running around it too, going the other way and trying to get away from me. I was checking the name tags and the SRO was Pete Schoeffel, who was the last guy to arrive at the table. Pete was a Navy Lt. Commander who was senior to me.

I looked across and saw Pete coming with his mother. I went over to him and took him by the shoulder. I pulled his head forward and told him, "Gene Wilbur is at our table."

Pete started to shake like a dog. "What the fuck is he doing there?"

"I have no idea, but you are the SRO. What are we going to do?"

We decided to freeze him out. "Don't talk to him," was the decision.

I went over to an Army sergeant POW assigned to our table with his date, who was also Army Corporal, and snarled, "Sergeant, I am giving you a direct order. You are not to talk to this Navy captain. Do you understand me?"

He was shocked. He had no idea what was going on. He answered, "Yes sir, I understand."

I turned to the WAC and told her, "You too corporal. Not a word."

Wilber is standing there with his mouth hanging open and his wife who was aghast at the whole thing, and then Admiral

Zumwalt came in with his wife, who as you may recall was a white Russian. She spoke with a little bit of an accent, and she was very pleasant.

It was obvious that no one was going to talk to Wilbur. Zumwalt was so mad about the dinner situation that he went back to the Pentagon afterward and really raised hell with his staff about why Wilbur was at the table, and he didn't know about it.

Of course, they all knew. It was because we had already put the finger on Wilbur and Miller. The Secret Service had put them there because they didn't want any problems. We didn't have any problems, but we froze him out.

A few days later I was back at Tucson, and Admiral Stockdale called me up and asked me how we had handled it. I told him what Pete had told us to do and he said, "That's fine."

Chapter 14★ Preparing for War

I ATTENDED THE AIR COMMAND and Staff College in 1966, the year before I went to Vietnam. I went down there absolutely determined to be a distinguished graduate. I wanted that so badly, because I had such a difficult time as a young officer when I started pilot training. I wanted to really do well at the school to prove myself. I had performed fine in my follow-on F-100 training, but I was always trying to catch up, because in basic pilot training I often got airsick while doing acrobatics.

Anyhow, I went down there with the idea that I was going to perform great at Command and Staff College. I worked at it so hard, and I got so nervous at it that I actually developed shingles. I didn't even know what they were, but I soon learned. Shingles is a nervous affliction that is extremely painful. I had never had anything like that before.

I met some great classmates One of my former students in the F-100 was there, Jim Abrahmson. He was in my class and was selected for major early. Jim ultimately retired as a Lt. General. Jim Amon and Dick Secord were in my class. Those two guys ran around in Africa and through some other third world countries stealing more stuff from the communists than the law allows. Both of them made major general out of the deal.

Amon looked like a con man. He was really a tough, capable guy, and Secord looked exactly like a church choirboy. Mike Sullivan who later was the wing commander of the 354th at Myrtle Beach was in that class.

George Green was a pilot who had come out of a different aircraft in the Strategic Air Command. We managed to get him into that class, and he was one of my classmates in my F-4 class at Davis Monthan.

One day later, Green was scheduled to be in an ACM (Air Combat Maneuvering) flight, flying Number Two on Robin Olds' wing. He asked me, "What in the world do I do?"

I told him that he had to work really hard to be constantly cutting Olds off to be able to stay inside of him. When George got back on the ground and I asked him, "How did it go?"

He said that it had gone great. "I kept him in sight the whole flight."

That made me laugh.

Ken Haff was in that class. He was a West Point graduate and became one of my great friends. We went through F-4 training together, and later he was my roommate at Ubon in Thailand. He had been a SAC KC-135 pilot, and when they put him into F-4s, he had some problems with it. He was a good guy.

Dick Vogel, who was later a fellow POW, was in that class. Also, Chet Eby, and a navigator by the name of Don Kellum. Kellum was a really bright guy and a computer whiz. He later became my director of plans at 9th Air Force. He did all the planning and groundwork for what later became Desert Storm. Kellum, to my amazement, is still alive as I write this today. He smokes two or three packs of cigarettes a day and looks like he's ready to blow away at any moment.

One of the brightest guys in my class was a fellow by the name of John Sell. John had come to us from the Pentagon, and was a very quiet guy, prematurely balding and kind of wizened. One day I commented about one of our classmates, saying that he acted as though he knew where the bodies were buried. I'll never forget John's reply.

He looked at me and said, "Hell, he doesn't even know where the cemetery is." I had never heard that before. He was an extremely bright guy and a lot of fun.

Harry Pollack was one of the most unbelievable characters I've ever met. I saw him last year at the River Rats reunion at Seymore Johnson AFB. Harry had been experiencing combat since he was 9 years old, fighting the Germans in Poland. He ended up riding around Germany and Poland on a tank. In Vietnam, Harry was an F-105 pilot. He was flying out of Korat or Takhli, and I once heard him talking. He has a very distinct accent. I heard him say as he rolled in on the target, "After them, men."

I called out over the radio, "Go get'em, Harry." He was a good fellow.

My first wife Verna is one of my best friends to this day. She's a Scottish girl and the mother of my three boys. She lives in Tucson now. She and I had never lived in the South before this school. I had traveled a little bit, flying in and out of places, but I didn't know anything about it. We got a house out in the community, a rental home, with a large family room. We had two boys, Steven and Glenn with us. Douglas later came along.

We had a native Alabamian living to the right of us and another one living on the left. The native on the left was in the Navy Reserve, and he was friendly. In fact, both neighbors were pleasant enough.

That was the year that Martin Luther King made that march from Selma. I'll tell you things were really tense down there. I made some kind of comment about it, and my neighbor said something about how I wouldn't understand, because I was a Yankee.

I said, "Don't you see the plates on my car? I'm from Oregon."

He replied, "That doesn't make any difference. That's north of the Mason Dixon line. Therefore, you're a Yankee, and that's what you will stay."

I thought, "Boy oh boy, that's going to take some getting used to."

And of course it has. I now live in the deep South, in South Carolina. I've been there since 1978, and I now believe that I understand the Southerners as well as they understand themselves.

Later the assignments came in, and I was selected to go to F-4 training. I called Verna, and I was pretty excited about it. She said, "Well, I'm sure that will make you happy," but she was not pleased. However, we had known that in all probability I was going to be assigned to either F-4s or F-105s. I didn't think I'd get picked for F-100s, but I could have been and sent to South Vietnam, because I had about 1500 hours in the airplane. I was really excited to get picked for the F-4, and off we went to Davis Monthan AFB at Tucson for the transition. We moved in, and I promptly met Chappie James who was the deputy for operations (DO) and Jones Bolt. Jones was the wing commander. He now lives in Myrtle Beach.

I had and have tremendous respect for Jones Bolt. Chappie was a different case. I was fond of him personally, and he was on the phone to me when I got off the airplane at March. While I liked Chappie, I didn't believe he was a very good pilot.

In Thailand, Robin Olds got the message about Chappie pretty soon. After one mission in which he flat froze, Robin never let him go up North again without an IP in the back seat. Bill Kirk often got the duty of keeping Chappie out of trouble. Kirk got to fly with him a good bit.

After I came home, on my first accident investigation, I was up at Luke AFB investigating an F-104 accident. At the time, when I was the assistant DO of the 355th Tac Fighter Wing at Tucson.

One of the captains at Luke introduced me to another young officer at the officer's club bar. "Colonel, this is Danny James," he said.

I stuck my hand out and said, "Hi Danny, nice to meet you."

We continued with our conversation, and the captain again said, "Sir, that's General Chappie James' son."

I turned to him, and I said, "So what?" I'll never forget the look on Danny James' face.

He leaned to me, and he said, "Colonel, thank you very much."

I really meant it too. I wanted him to stand on his own two feet. I knew he wanted that, too. He didn't need any help from his father. Danny is now a Lieutenant General in the Air National Guard

Mrs. James was one of the nicest ladies I ever met in my life. I thought the world of her and felt the same way about her son Danny.

When we started training at Davis Monthan AFB, Arizona, in the F-4, I was impressed with the airplane. It had a tremendous amount of power. You could turn it pretty well, and it didn't bleed off energy in the turn like the F-100 did. The IP's kept telling me that it would depart on you, or that the bottom would fall right out from underneath you if you weren't careful.

I asked the instructor pilot, or IP, who was telling me that, "Did you ever fly the F-100?"

He said no, and that didn't surprise me. I told him that the F-100 will depart on you with the speed of light, and I don't think this airplane's going to be that bad. Of course, it wasn't. The F-4 was easy to fly and nowhere near as unforgiving as the F-100 was. I thought the F-4 was a very honest airplane. It told you what you needed to know when you needed to know it, and it carried a big bomb load. In the hands of a competent fighter pilot, it was as accurate in gunnery as the F-100. However, the F-4 had a poor reputation in Vietnam because the quality of the pilots assigned to it was not good across the board. The plane could also carry Sidewinders and Sparrow missiles for air-to-air combat. Sometimes a 20-millimeter Gatling gun was hung on the centerline station, and in that configuration especially, it was certainly more than adequate.

Most MiG kills by Air Force F-4s were accomplished using the radar guided Sparrow missiles, but a number were shot down with the gun. Darrel "Big D" Simmons shot down two MiG-17s with the gun on a single mission. The F-4 wouldn't out turn the MiGs, but you could certainly go into the vertical with them using superior power and do all right, so that was positive.

I enjoyed flying it. I was in D.O. William's squadron. Ron Parks was the ops officer. We had a fair amount of F-100 experience. With Buddy Mentor, Ron Christianson, Rolly Moore and myself, we had thousands of hours F-100 IP experience between us, and we really didn't need to be watched that closely by the instructors. In fact, we had way more fighter experience than the IPs who had taught us at DM.

They got experience from us, and we got knowledge from them. It was a good trade off. I enjoyed the time there. I got my wife and family set up. By that time my third boy had come along, and we were in an apartment out on Golf Links Road. After six months training there, I set sail for Ubon, Thailand.

Chapter 15★ The Raid

IN SEPTEMBER OF 1970, THE guards had us roll up and moved us out to a place we called Camp Faith. There were POWs there from the Plantation, Son Tay, the Annex, and the Zoo. They had moved all of these guys from outlying prisons with the exception of those who were being held down at the Hanoi Hilton.

So, there we were. The building was very nice, and we were all in one big place out in the country. We had a courtyard. We could go out there and walk around when we were allowed. For the first few days, they didn't let all the rooms out together. I guess they were worried about having some kind of riot on their hands.

We discovered very quickly that there were POWs from all over. We were climbing up on the walls and waving to them. The Vietnamese would get upset if they caught us doing that but not to the point of beating the hell out of everybody.

This was like a World War II Stalag, much more of a classic type of prison camp than we had ever seen before. There were no individual rooms. There were no torture rooms. There was none of that. They came in with the food, and we handled the distribution and served it up ourselves.

They would show up at the gate with big pots of food. Our guys would carry it in and dish it out. Afterwards, we would wash our dishes. At night they would come around and say, "OK, it's time to close the blinds." They'd actually start to turn off some of the lights. They'd turn lights off, and then the guards would come by on the porch and look in with flashlights. It was a lot quieter there. We were out of the city. We had no idea in the world where, but we knew it was somewhere west of Hanoi. It was much more relaxed and actually kind of nice after what we had been through.

This was unbelievable to us, because we had been sleeping with a naked light bulb for the entire duration that we were

POWs. I'd been up there since 1967, and I'd never spent a single night without having a light over my head shining down on me. We thought that we would be there at Camp Faith for the duration if all went well.

But all didn't go well. There came the night of the Son Tay raid. If you haven't read the book, "The Raid," I can't recommend it too highly. (The Raid: The Son Tay Prison Rescue Mission, by Benjamin F. Shemmer)

I've been around some tough men in my life, but the Son Tay Raiders were a class above and beyond. They came in to rescue us in November 1970. I met some of these men at a joint reunion with them down at Fort Walton Beach a couple of years ago. They are truly different.

I've been up close and personal with them, and I mean these guys look like they'd kill you right now. They were pleasant and all, but they were really a bunch of tough monkeys.

They came into North Vietnam, and with any luck at all, they would have taken out some POWs. The only reason they didn't was that the Son Tay prison had been emptied shortly before the raid for unknown reasons.

That night, I woke up to the roar of an F-4 going by overhead. I rolled out of bed and looked right over the top of the transom. I saw this F-4 Phantom go screaming by. He had both afterburners going. It was a moonlit night, and I could have read a newspaper out there it was so clear. Surface-to-air missiles were going by really low. It was really something to behold.

I thought, "My God, what in the world is going on?" Lyndon Johnson stopped the bombing in 1968, and he didn't even get a prisoner count in exchange for it. He got nothing for it, and that is one more thing I will never forgive him for.

Nonetheless, here we had our fighters up there drilling around. I saw an F-105 go by. It was pretty exciting stuff. I thought, "What the hell is happening?"

As it turned out, they were only about eight or ten miles away at Son Tay. Had they known to come down a little bit further, they would have found a bunch of us. There were over two hundred prisoners there with me. But we had been moved there so recently that our intelligence hadn't discovered we were there.

The Vietnamese had a terrible time trying to keep secrets and telling the truth. They broadcasted on Hanoi radio, acknowledging that there had been a raid. I can't remember what they called it, but we knew there had obviously been some kind of raid into North Vietnam. They claimed they had captured a number of pirates, and that they had killed a bunch more. They claimed to have shot down dozens of airplanes, but we knew that was all bullshit. As it turned out, they were talking about the Son Tay raid.

In actual fact, the sole America casualty suffered by the Son Tay raiders was a single broken ankle that occurred when one of the helicopters was deliberately crashed into the middle of the Son Tay compound. That was the only way the raiders felt they could get in there and have total surprise.

The guards didn't tell us much; however, it became apparent after a week or two that there had been a rescue attempt, and that this operation had garnered the sincere attention of the North Vietnamese. Their "blue chips" had been truly threatened.

After the raid, they moved us all together where they could keep closer track of us. This turned out to be a tremendous benefit to us, because now we were able to really get organized. They had seven big rooms and a lot of little rooms in a place we called Rawhide. I started off in room number one while most of the senior guys were in room number six. That was where Risner, Stockdale, Denton, and a bunch of the older guys, and I mean older in terms of both age and rank, were held.

The Son Tay raiders were devastated that they hadn't been able to get any of us out of prison. I talked to some of them in Fort Walton Beach, Florida. Ross Perot brought a bunch of them to meet some of us. We have been telling them for years that their actions spawned the birth and the growth of the 4th Allied POW Wing, because we had never ever been put in one place together until the aftermath of that raid.

Chapter 16★ Back to Hanoi –Birth of the 4th Allied POW Wing

THE SON TAY RAIDERS came in on the night of November 21, 1970. The next day, we remained there in the Faith prison, but the night after that, the Vietnamese came with trucks and emptied that area. They took every swinging dick down to Hanoi, and we were all crammed into the big prison.

In Hanoi, I had a personal lying down space measuring 16 inches by 72 inches in the room where I was placed. We were crammed in like sardines. They moved a bunch of Vietnamese prisoners out and put us into what we called Camp Unity.

That resulted in creation of the 4th Allied POW Wing, and it came about thanks to the Son Tay raiders. The raid scared the North Vietnamese so badly, they put us all together in that big prison where they could watch us.

As Orson Swindle once said, there were so many troublemakers in there that you had to get in line to get make mischief. It was really kind of funny, but we started right off saying, "We're going to take control." The real organization didn't start at that moment, however. That came a little later, and it happened after we decided we'd have church services.

For some reason or the other, I didn't ever quite figure out why, the Vietnamese said, "No, you are not going to have church services. We are not going to have that many people getting together in the middle of a room." Well, we were all in the room anyhow, but they indicated that they were not going to put up with it. There's not going to be a choir singing and so on.

We were all crammed in this one little room, and it was crazy that they would get so upset about it, but they did. We would not back off. We went ahead and had the church services and sang. They came into room 6 where the seniors were with guards, and they did something that was very unusual. Jailers don't normally want to bring guns into a prison. Guards with guns can be overcome, the guns seized, and then there really could be trouble.

The Vietnamese came in this time with armed guards. It indicated how truly upset they were, because they had never before brought armed soldiers into any of our camps. These were strangers, armed soldiers with AK-47s and they looked pretty capable. They were loaded for bear, ready to go, and they weren't kidding.

They started removing the senior guys. They took Robbie Risner out first. The guys started to sing the Star-Spangled Banner, and you could hear it all over that section of Hanoi. We all joined in of course, and it was a roaring rendition of the National Anthem. Risner went out, and he said he felt nine feet tall. Ross Perot got hold of that comment years later. There is now a statue of Risner on the grounds of the Air Force Academy that stands nine feet tall. That came from what Robbie said that day.

Next, they took Stockdale out and then Denton. Then Bud Day was hauled out along with some other colonels and lieutenant colonels and thrown into Rawhide. Several collaborators also went over there. Once all that rank was together, they began to formalize the rules and regulations of the 4th Allied POW Wing. For security reasons, we called these rules "plums" as in the fruit.

When the Vietnamese told us that we couldn't have a church service, the brass decided that we would go on a hunger strike. There is nothing more serious in an oriental prison than to go on a hunger strike. I think our senior guys knew that, and it was the reason for it. If the senior officers told us to go on a hunger strike, we would quit eating.

The Vietnamese countered the hunger strike rather quickly by coming in with a couple of meals and then removing all of the water. That is a pretty good way to break a hunger strike. Some of the guys were already pretty sick including Dave Burrows, and they knew that. Burrows was given a cup of water from time to time. The Vietnamese were dead serious. They wanted the hunger strike stopped.

They were the ones who told us we couldn't have a church service. The fact that we were having a hunger strike to protest this apparently found its way downtown to the hierarchy of the Army who was in charge of us. Somebody probably said, "You dumb bastards, what are you doing telling them they can't have a church service? That's crazy."

Pretty soon, they came in with a statement and read it us on the squawk box. "Attention the whole camp." We were all sitting in our rooms, listening. One of their English speakers read this thing that said, "Of course we will allow church services, and of course we will allow religion, of course because we are tolerant," and on and on.

I'm sure someone downtown got mad as hell at the camp authority for being so damned dumb by prohibiting church services. They also said there could be only four people singing at one time and to keep the noise down. That's really what they were after, I think. They were afraid that we would be singing something that could be heard on the outside of the prison, and that we could be communicating with the outside world. They weren't going to tolerate that.

So that is how our group church services got started. The seniors started sending out rules and regulations, directions. We named our organization the "4th Allied POW Wing." It was designated the 4th Wing because it was the fourth war in modern times involving America, during which prisoners were taken, beginning with the First World War. It included the Second World War, Korea, and now Vietnam.

It was "Allied" because our overall group included one South Vietnamese Air Force pilot. His name was Dat Nguyen. We also had two Thai Air Force guys with us. One was a pilot, an officer, and the other was a sergeant. Those two guys had been flying supplies into a place near Dien Bien Phu in some kind of a prop transport airplane when the damn thing had an engine failure. They crash-landed and got scooped up. They were never put in with us, but despite our separation from them, we felt a kinship to them. We would see them out sweeping and doing bits and pieces. To the best of my knowledge, they were not mistreated, or if they were, we never saw it.

The Vietnamese seemed to just leave them alone. They kept their distance from us, too. They were very careful not to get caught communicating with us, though we learned that both of those Thais could speak English. Later, many years ago, both of them came to the United States. I helped host one Thai officer who was a colonel by then.

That was the origin of the 4th APW. Charlie Plumb and I talked about it a good bit, and we proposed a design for our Wing Standard. The motif is an eagle shackled with a chain. It was placed on several different book covers with the motto, "Return with Honor." Charlie did the main part of the work. I helped.

Colonel John Flynn was the first commander of the wing. He was designated "Wing Commander in Perpetuity." We only had one. Colonel Robbie Risner was the Wing Vice Commander. He was shot down in 1965, and when the colonel's list came out later that year, he was on it. He was promoted early, so he outranked Norm Gaddis and Colonels Bean and Wynn. None of us got a vote or were asked, and that was fine by me.

We also had three enlisted guys with us. The three were captured in 1965. They were crewmen on an Air Force helicopter that came up there in a rescue attempt. There were five in the crew, the pilot, copilot and three enlisted men, all of whom were captured. When they were taken prisoner, Art Cornier was a staff sergeant, Bill Robinson was an airman first class, and the third one, Turner I think, was an airman second class.

Someone decided that it would be a great idea if we put these guys through OCS (Officer Candidate School). After an enormous amount of tapping back and forth through the walls, we designed a syllabus.

We passed the information up the line to the hierarchy of the 4th APW, and the leaders blessed the concept and the syllabus. These guys finished the program in about two or three years, and they were given battlefield commissions as second lieutenants.

When Colonel Flynn returned home in 1973, he had an audience with the Air Force Chief of Staff, "Three Fingered" Jack Ryan. Flynn had a whole laundry list of things to talk about.

There were OERs (Officer's Effectiveness Reports) to accomplish along with a lot of other items to be discussed. One of those items was that we had conducted an OCS program, and that we'd given battlefield commissions to these three (now) lieutenants.

General Ryan looked at him and said, "John, tell me, why are there battlefield commissions?"

Flynn mumbled something, and then Ryan told him, "The reason for battlefield commissions is to replenish a shortage of officers. In your case, never have so few been led by so many."

"That's true, General Ryan, but I promised these guys."

Ryan finally gave in, "You got it." He gave them the commissions.

As it turned out, by the time we got released, Art Cornier, who had been a POW for eight years, had a line number for chief master sergeant. He said, "I'm not going to go from being a chief master sergeant to a second lieutenant," and he refused the commission. He became the NCOIC of the survival school up in Spokane. The other two, Robinson and Turner, both said they wanted to go to flight school. The Air Force made that happen though both of them were over the official age limit.

Robbie went into flight school and, as it turned out, he could not fly an airplane solo. Try as they might, he just couldn't do it. They gave him something like double the normal number of rides trying to get him to the point where he was safe to solo. Finally, they told him, "Robbie, it just isn't going to work." He agreed, and I believe he eventually retired as a captain.

Turner made it through pilot training, became a major and did a great job. Occasionally, I see him down at Pensacola for our annual physical. Several more enlisted guys came in with us when the B-52s started to bomb near Hanoi in the 1972 Linebacker operation. However, that was well after the time we had been in the OCS business.

Chapter 17★ Passing Time

AS I SAID BEFORE, FOR most of the time I was in jail, each of us had about sixteen inches of space to lie down in and about seventy inches in length. I came down with colds often during the winters there and became really ill at times. We had lost a lot of weight, and we just couldn't keep warm.

We had some really course paper that we used to wipe our tails. We were given some extra paper, so we could make what we called a "punk." If you rolled the paper tight enough, you could light the punk, and it would sit there and smolder for hours. That was one little concession they made.

We would light the punk, and it would smolder. The guys could light cigarettes off of it. At one point, we were given up to six cigarettes a day. Some of the guys got together and started picking up the butts, recycling the tobacco. They'd put the tobacco into any kind of paper and smoked them. Four of that group died of lung cancer in later years.

One late night, Don Waltman, who was one of the funniest men I ever met, was sitting down next to his net talking to Ed Hubbard, who was under his.

Finally, someone growled, "For God's sake, go to sleep."

Don said, "OK, I'm going to put the punk out. Does anyone want a cigarette before I put it out?" There was total silence.

So, he stated again, "I'm gonna put the punk out."

Again, total silence.

"Last call. I'm gonna put the punk out."

Absolute silence.

Then he said in a loud, very deep, bass voice, "Fuck it. I think I'll have a cigarette."

And of course, the whole room came unglued, laughing. That startled the guards. They came over and started banging on the doors. We still had a little bit of humor in us.

One day, one of the guys got pink eye. The guards came in with some eye drops. They were going to give everybody eye drops. Lou Shattock had lost an eye when he was shot down, and he declined the drops. He would not let them give him the drops in his remaining eye and fought them off.

I thought the drops might help. So, I took the drops. The whole damn room got pink eye except Lou. They were using a contaminated dropper. They were touching infected areas with it. It was really a bitch, but it finally passed.

We instituted a lot of education classes. There were some very smart guys in there. Dave Brose had been an instructor at the Air Force Academy and had a masters' degree. George Hall was an expert in the French language, and we had a few guys who could speak German fluently. There were others who were experts in different subjects as well.

We all had favorite stories that we related. I told the story of "Gone with the Wind," by Margaret Mitchell. I got a supporting cast to help me tell the story, playing different roles. We could take a movie, chop it up in four or five sections, and it would last for an hour or more. It was like a movie coming to town back home. Everybody would gather around and listen to me tell the story of Gone with the Wind and several other books that I had read. We told each other stories, and we had movie nights.

We didn't have any paper to write on. The Vietnamese finally gave us a little chalk, so the guys teaching the math classes would do their figures on the concrete.

We finally started getting some packages from home, but the North Vietnamese raided them. They thought the candy was pretty good and kept it, but they did let some One-a-Day vitamins come in. I had no idea how run down I was until I took six or so of those vitamins, one at a time on consecutive days. I felt like I was walking on cloud nine after that.

I guess the people sending us the packages were members of the Defense Intelligence Agency. They were including in there some special items. In the grape Lifesavers, they had included little packages of very tiny dots. There was a little magnifying device that you put the dots in and read what was sent. Those were hidden in the Wilson Meat Bars.

We were able to get the dots out of the grape LifeSavers and put them into the little magnifying glass. It was similar to the things that were sold in Japan to look at dirty pictures with. You could hold it up to the light and read what was written there. It was incredible. They took an eight by eleven page and shrunk it down to the size of a period on a typewritten page. It was very small and if you dropped it, you would have a hell of a time finding it.

We would dissolve the grape Lifesavers in water. The water had to be in a cup, or you would lose the package of dots. The information on the dots had all kinds of news, football score, promotion lists, things like that, none of which, if discovered, would be tantamount to violating the Geneva Convention. We never got a thing that had information about locations or maps that could be used to accuse us of a violation of the Geneva Convention.

That was good because the Vietnamese were sampling the goods. One day one of them bit down on a Wilson Meat Bar and out popped a magnifying device. Evidently, they also found a package of dots, blew it up, and read it.

They came in and shook the place down. They gave us one of the most complete shakedowns we had ever had. It was just before Christmas and they took everything out that we had. They took all our decorations, and it was one of the low points of all the time I was in jail.

They also took all our playing cards. You could take some of those cards and put them into water and there would be readable information there, like promotion lists, dates of rank and so forth. The Vietnamese didn't appreciate it though. We never got any pictures after, that but we occasionally got mail. Packages were still coming in though. One of the more popular guards, Mumbles, could speak some English. He told us "Packages very good. We appreciate." They were helping themselves to all our stuff that came in.

Some of the guys were sending mail out with clandestine messages in them. They communicated to our folks to stop sending the hidden stuff. I had never been trained on how to send clandestine mail. I guess one out of every twenty or thirty who go through survival school get this training.

I was still able to write a letter about every one or two months. Jim Hickerson came to me and asked me if I would learn the clandestine mail system, because I was a regular recipient of mail. I was afraid that would result in me losing that privilege. I was concerned for my family's sake, because they had not heard anything from me for the first two years I was there. So, I declined. It was a mistake that I have always regretted.

Later, I was part of the covert committee, and hopefully, I made up for it. I should have put the prisoners, who were my brothers, ahead of my family. I have always felt badly about that.

Those rooms could really be hot. One day around 1971, they came in with a tall ladder. They set up wiring and installing a fan, one fan in this big cell block. I thought that when they turned it on the air would really start moving, but when it started, the blades were barely moving. I said to myself, "Shit, this is a waste of time and effort. That will never work." Boy, was I wrong.

That fan made all the difference in the world by just barely moving the air around. Whenever the electricity would go off, sweat would just pop right out of us. Those people had lived there all their lives and really did know about fans.

One day in May of 1972, we were sitting around when an air raid started. We had been there so long that we didn't really pay any attention to it. Then the fighters got into it, MiGs and the F- 4s, and you could hear the burners going in and out. The guns stopped, and the SAMs stopped. There was just a big dogfight between the MiGs and the F- 4s right over the top of Hanoi. One of the ways that both the MiGs and the F- 4s would get their adversary off their tail was to drop down over the city, going over it as fast as they could go.

Of course, everybody down there on the ground carried an AK, and they would shoot at the F- 4s. However, sometimes the second fighter would get shot. They would fire at the noise and hit the second guy. I was sitting there in the room, and suddenly, there was an enormous crackling boom. An F-4 went over in full afterburners. The boom lifted cups up, it lifted dirt up, and it lifted me up. The compression of that sonic boom was unbelievable. I talked to the pilot who was flying that Phantom later, and he told me that he was going Mach 1.2 right over the top of the prison.

I looked down the cell block and saw a big piece of ceiling, about the size of a blanket, break loose and came tumbling down on top of Jim Young. He was sitting there with three other guys playing bridge. Blood started running down his face and out of his nose. He had really been hit hard. He just leaned forward and said, "Four hearts." The Vietnamese came racing in and got a doctor, but none of it fazed him. It was obvious we had been there way too long.

Our South Vietnamese POW, Dat Nguyen, an A-1H pilot we called "Max," was fluent in French, English and of course, Vietnamese. He could understand what the guards were talking about because he had been born in Hanoi.

One day he told us the guards were saying we were all going to be moved out of Hanoi. They were going to move half of us to a camp called Cao Bang, up by the Chinese border, and the other half to Long Song, also near that border. They came in that night, our whole room got rolled up, and we were loaded into some trucks.

We rode in those trucks for about thirty-six hours, and I was really afraid that a flight of F-105s would come by and shoot the hell out of the convoy. Fortunately, we were lucky, and that didn't happen. They drove up a very narrow trail, and then the convoy of about twenty trucks stopped, and we were offloaded. There was lots of yelling and shouting as we went into empty buildings. There was no electricity, just lanterns. I heard the guards yelling and hollering in one building, and they came out with a big pole. A huge snake, about eight or nine feet long, dangled on the end of it.

We had arrived at what we soon called Dogpatch. We were up on the border with China. I had no idea that the camp was there. However, some guys had been told earlier that they were building a camp to put people in who would stay there the rest of their lives. It was built way out in the Karst mountains, and the Vietnamese were threatening the local people that they had better behave or that would be their fate.

It appeared that construction had been started on the camp, but that it had ceased in 1969. We could only assume that they stopped working on it when Ho Chi Minh died. Here we were in 1972, and it was obviously a backup camp to put prisoners in. There was no electricity and no running water. We were in the middle of nowhere in the karst mountains. We had no idea whether anyone knew where we were or knew anything about us.

NGÀY VIẾT (Dated) 23 Dec. 1972

Dear Folks, Merry Christmas and a Happy New Year. I cannot tell you how proud I am of you both. Dads latest achievement is wonderful. Greatly enjoyed reading Moms few lines in Vernas letter. Please continue to do this. The constant help you have been to Verna is a source of constant comfort to me and I shall be eternally grateful to you both. Have Verna put two jars of freeze-dried coffee in each package.

Love Jack

GHI CHÚ (N.B.):

1. Phải viết rõ và chỉ được viết trên những dòng kẻ sẵn (*Write legibly and only on the lines*).
2. Gia đình gửi đến cũng phải theo đúng mẫu, khuôn khổ và quy định này (*Notes from families should also conform to this proforma*).

Chapter 18★ Dogpatch and Linebacker

THE DOGPATCH CAMP WAS JUST outside Cao Bang, right on the China border. It held a bit more than two hundred of us. There were around eighteen to nineteen guys to a building with a couple of the blocks containing twenty-one. We went right to work setting up methods of communications between all the buildings, and it didn't take very long to complete the process.

We were sitting way up there against the mountains knowing full well that it would be a very difficult place to come and get us. I'm sure that is why the North Vietnamese built it there.

The only way anyone could have gotten there from Laos would have been to use tankers and refuel helicopters two or three times on the way. They would likely have had to preposition some supplies. It never came to that, as things turned out, but I'm sure there were people looking into it. We believed they could find us, if it became necessary. We felt certain that the intelligence would learn that we had moved out.

About five or six days later, we heard a terrific sonic boom. We thought that it was an SR-71 going by, and I thought, "Well, they're up here looking for us anyhow.

About three or four days after that, there was a double boom, and we figured that they had put two of them up there, and they were telling us that they knew where we were. That was a pretty happy day. We were a long way from nowhere.

We were being fed reasonably well. One day they actually came in with some beef. One of the guys saw that they had brought a hindquarter of an oxen and put that together with some kind of BBQ sauce. It was pretty damned good. I hadn't had a piece of beef like that in all the years I had been up there. It was very welcome.

The villagers from across the way would appear at the gate, and the guards would barter with them with beads and clothing. I doubt that the Vietnamese money available down in Hanoi was of much use up there.

Originally, I was in building seven with Kyle Berg, the greatest Hollywood gin player I had ever met in my life at that point. I used to think that damn guy had mirrors placed around somewhere. I stayed there in that building for around three or four months until they moved me to building thirteen. I was the SRO for the first time in that place.

It became apparent to us that the Vietnamese were getting us sorted out. We could see that we were getting placed by date of capture, and we felt that we knew exactly what they were doing. They were setting us up for release, and that helped raise moral enormously.

There was a small courtyard outside of our building with a cistern there where we could bath. It was cold in the winter, and I remember that we knocked a thick layer of ice off the surface of the water in the cistern there one morning.

We kept wondering what it was that triggered the decision to move us up there. We eventually learned from Dat (Max) that he had overheard them saying that the Vietnamese had seen at least one aircraft carrier with a whole bunch of great big helicopters on it north of Latitude 1900 North. The furthest north American carriers had ever gone before was 1900, and now our government had moved them up past that point.

We thought then that the Vietnamese were convinced there was a rescue attempt coming into Hanoi and had therefore moved us. They tried to choreograph the travel in such a way that photography would show no change, because they knew we had drones coming by from time to time to take pictures of the prison.

The second group never left Hanoi. The North Vietnamese finally realized after a few days that the big helicopters were gunships brought in to shoot up the barge traffic. By this time, we had blockaded Haiphong.

Each of our buildings had two large rooms, one at each end, and two smaller rooms to the right and left of the hall as you walked down from one large room to the other. The larger rooms held about seven or eight per room. There was just a single guy in each of the small rooms. They'd put one guy in there at night when they locked us down, but they didn't give us a choice on who stayed in those small rooms. They decided on a day-to-day basis who was going where and when.

It wasn't any great hardship for someone to stay in the single facility. They locked down the entire building every night. They were very scrupulous about that. They also held a head count the moment they opened the door in the morning to make sure everybody was still there.

There was one small window in each of the big rooms. It was not really a window, just an aperture with bars in it, so that you couldn't possibly crawl through. Even if there had been no bars, it would have been almost impossible to crawl through, and they were high up on the wall. It was very difficult to get up and look out. However, we found that if one of us got down on his hands and knees it was possible for another guy to stand on his back and see out.

We wanted to communicate out those windows, and we did so at every opportunity. While outside, we could see the other buildings by climbing up on the fence around the little courtyard. We could make contact with those folks, too.

Occasionally, one of the North Vietnamese would call us out and ask us how things were going. It was the same old bullshit; how's the food, how's this, and how's that? But by and large, they pretty much left us alone. In some ways that became a source of frustration, because the Vietnamese were the only sources of information we had. The only way we could find out what was going on was from the guards or officers at a quiz.

They'd turn on the camp radio at times, and there were speakers in every building that they could play it through. We could occasionally listen to Hanoi Radio, but not very often.

I had a standing bet of one martini with Mickey McCuistion that something would happen that would herald our release on or before the 20th of January 1973. My reasoning was that Nixon had a four-year term of office, and he had to have a plan to get us out of there prior to the end of his term. That is what I based it on.

We were all in our buildings when the Vietnamese came around on Christmas of 1972. They would generally visit us on Christmas and there would be a little bit of a "special" treat, maybe an orange or something like that. They'd say that the priest sends this as praise for peace, all that kind of crap.

This time they came around on Christmas Eve. There was one officer and three enlisted guards. The officer had a little bit of candy, and he tried to pull off the congeniality act, but just couldn't do it. He and his three subordinates were so pissed off that they just couldn't hide it. Normally they could get pretty greasy around Christmas and Tet, but this time they couldn't hide their anger.

I said to them that I would appreciate if they would not lock us down until we had time for church service. The officer said, "How much time?"

I replied, "Forty-five minutes." Our church service took about one minute, but I said forty-five minutes.

He looked at me and snarled, "I give you ten minutes," and then he slammed the door so damn hard the wall shook. They were really upset.

Of course, we had no idea at that time why they were so mad. The next day was Christmas day. The guards and the officer were acting very solemn. They served us a special Christmas meal which was pretty bad. We all kind of wondered, "What the hell is going on?" Anytime they were that mad, it was good for us, but we didn't know what had caused their anger.

Come the morning of the twenty-sixth, the officer and guard came by to let us out for bathing. They opened the door and made a washing motion, and we all went out into the courtyard.

We had been out there maybe ten minutes and another guard arrived. One of my guys was sitting on the ground leaning up against the wall, and the guard yelled at him to stand up and bow. Well, we had stopped bowing at least two years before. They had told us not to bow after Ho died.

I thought, "What the hell's the matter with them, screaming at my guy?"

The guard slammed the damn door, the outside door to the courtyard and ran away. Pretty soon he came back and said, "Be," meaning me. I was the senior guy in the room, and they knew who the hell the senior guys were.

He gave me the signal, the little chop sign on the wrist meaning to put on my long reds, and that we were going to go talk to an officer. I was really curious to know what it was that set all of this off.

He took me off to a quiz room. The Rat waited there. He started yelling at me about how my guy hadn't bowed. I thought what the hell, and I started to yell back at him. I'm here to tell you that took all the courage I had at that point in time.

I really wanted to know what was happening. I said, "We haven't stood up and bowed for years. What the hell is bothering you?"

The Rat reached down and got a newspaper. He slammed it down on the table in front of me. There was a picture of six nice, round-faced Caucasians. He hollered, "POWs, POWs, B-52 bomb Hanoi, B-52 bomb Hanoi."

"I don't believe you." That was the standard answer we used to try to get more facts.

He said, "B-52 start on the sixteenth," something like that, and he told me the damned B-52s had been bombing down there for over a week, which of course just tickled the shit out of me.

Finally, he told me, "Go back to your building and tell your men behave."

So, I went back and told them, guys, "The B-52s are downtown. We're going home." We found out later that the name of the operation that brought the B-52s to Hanoi was Linebacker.

Earlier in the year, sometime around the end of October or first part of November, the camp radio had come on. The North Vietnamese read the nine major points of the agreement between the United States and North Vietnam as negotiated by Henry Kissinger and Le Due Tho. That is discussed in the book, "Kissinger," by Bernard and Marvin Kalb.

They read these nine points, and they all sounded reasonable to me.

Then they said that the renegade government in Saigon refused to sign, refused to agree to it, and that was true.

I thought, "Oh hell, this is really going to cause trouble." The guys were really down. It was like getting hit in the stomach with a hard blow, and it took our breath away.

The President was tough enough to hang in through all this, and he did. He tried but couldn't get Thieu to agree. Then, at that point, the North Vietnamese backed away from it.

That's when Nixon initiated Linebacker, the Christmas bombings of North Vietnam. He literally bombed them back to the table. There are people who don't agree with that, who will tell you that's not true, but the guys who were there, and who watched it, know that is exactly what happened.

It was around the nineteenth of January. I was sitting there playing cribbage with Mickey. Everybody knew about the bet between me and Mickey. I bet that we would have news about going home by the 20th of January. It was a famous bet in the building. He got up and wandered down to the other room. I turned to Hal Miniux and said, "If I had any guts at all, I'd double that bet right now."

"But Jack, tomorrow is the twentieth and nothing has happened."

I said, "I can't help it. I have this overwhelming feeling that something is about to happen." I really did. Just overwhelming that something was in the works, that something was about to happen.

The guards came by later on that day, and they locked the whole building down. It was bitter cold. We had arranged our beds. By this time, we had two blankets, and we had learned how to roll our mosquito nets up into the blankets to add a little insulation. We were all bedded down and had blown out our one little candle that we had in a tin can.

Then I heard them. I heard the trucks coming. The memory of it almost makes me want to cry sitting here now. I couldn't believe the emotions. It wasn't just a single truck. We had heard one or two trucks coming before. We could listen and tell that this was a whole convoy coming up there.

Miniux jumped up and got somebody there where he could stand on him and look out the window as the trucks came in. The truck lights shining across his face as they went by one by one. He counted twenty-one trucks. He looked down at me in amazement and asked, "How the hell did you know?"

I'll never forget that. I want to tell you I just had a gut feeling. It was obvious they were there to get us. The trucks got all lined up, and they waited during the day. The drivers slept during the day, and that night the guards came by and told us to roll up, that we were going back to Hanoi. We rolled up and went back, and that was the end of our stay up at Cao Bang.

Chapter 19★ Countdown to Leaving

WHEN WE WERE UP ON THE China border in November of 1972, back home the Presidential election was taking place. Richard Nixon was running against George McGovern. We had our own secret ballot election there in prison. There were a little more than two hundred men there.

When everything was tallied up, we found that the vote was around 185 for Nixon, and the votes for McGovern were somewhere in the neighborhood of 25.

One thing bothered me though. In one of our buildings, there were twenty-one men and of that number, nineteen of them voted for McGovern.

My great friend Charlie Plumb was in that building, part of my clandestine network. He told me that he and one other had voted for Nixon and the rest for McGovern. Morale wasn't all that it could have been in there, obviously.

There were a couple of guys in there who really had gotten sick and tired of the whole thing and wanted to just give up. They were all younger guys, all junior officers, and they had kind of bailed out on us. That affected the moral of everyone. I can tell you that Nixon was overwhelmingly the favorite of the POWs in the camp, even though McGovern said that he was going to get us out of that war.

The thing that bothered us about McGovern was that while he stated that he was going to bring us out, we were afraid that we would end up having to crawl home. Part of our motto was return with honor. The way McGovern talked made it sound very much like there wouldn't be any honor involved at all. We felt that he would beg to get us back. Then we would just quit and scuttle home like whipped puppies. I hadn't trusted Senator McGovern before, and I never saw any great reason why I should trust him then.

We found twenty-three other POWs in the Little Vegas part of the camp that we had not known were there. The SRO for that group was Ted Guy. We wanted to discover who the other twenty-two were and set out to do that on the morning of the third of March. Our crappers were holes in the ground that dropped down into honey buckets. There was a brick wall between the two holes, I crawled up on the brick wall between the two holes and shouted out the window. It had bars and barbed wire and all. Hal Monlux was in the crapper helping me.

I was using phonetic spelling with the names. I wanted to make sure I got them right. They started off giving me their names. Then he said there were four civilians one of whom was a woman, a German nurse. She had been captured in the 1968 Tet offensive at Hue.

She was picked up with two other nurses, both Americans, and the two of them sang like canaries. We heard them on the radio denouncing our government, denouncing everything imaginable. Finally, the Vietnamese let them go.

There was a German doctor, a Frenchman, and a Filipino. Most of the rest of them were enlisted guys. They started through the list, and then I heard the name, Floyd James Thompson.

I asked, "Is that Floyd Thompson?"

"Yes," came the answer.

Floyd Thompson was the first American captured in the war in Vietnam. He was grabbed in April of 1964. Ev Alverez was captured in August of 1964. Floyd should have been in the first group that had already been released based on the capture date, but there he was. I made certain that I had the right name.

I looked down at Monlux, and I said, "Damn, the ink isn't even dry on the agreement, and we've already found a violation." Everyone was supposed to be released in the order of capture.

We got most of the names. I had two names to go when it got too dark at the end of the day. We had constant interruptions, frequent danger signals. I had guys posted everywhere with mirrors who could look down the outside corridors and see the guards coming. I was up and down off that brick wall all day long. It was very slow, very laborious work plus it was hard to hear because the outer wall of the prison was there, and Hanoi is a very noisy place with a lot of racket always going on.

One of the guys came in and said, "Colonel Gaddis says to quiet down, you're too loud."

I thought, "My God, if Norm Gaddis can hear us, as deaf as he is, we really do need to turn the volume down."

We collected names that we had never heard of before. Hal was writing them down, and we were recruiting guys to memorize them. Hal was making his list on discarded pieces of cigarette paper.

The next morning, March 4th, when we got up, I started right off at first light to get the remaining two or three names. I was just about to get the last name when there was another danger signal, and I jumped down. The door of the latrine was jerked open and one of the guys said, "They just took Gaddis out. The Four-Power Commission is out there. I think we are going home. Hurry up."

I told him, "If Gaddis comes back before I finish, start a fight at the gate. I have to get that last name." By this time, we were really screaming. There was so much noise and confusion.

Sure enough, Norm came back too soon, and as requested, there was a fight at the gate. I jumped down in the midst of all this melee and walked out of the latrine. Monlux had written down all the names.

He asked me, "What do I do with this?"

"You stick it where the sun don't shine and don't lose it."

That's the way he carried the last two or three names out of Hanoi, stuck up his rear end.

We were taken out of our rooms and changed out of our prison garb. The North Vietnamese told us to dress in our going home clothes and we did. We got into some clothes they had for us to wear home. We had shoes for the first time in years, a cotton jacket, cotton shirt, and cotton pants. We put everything on.

Representatives of the Four Power Commission were there. The Poles, the Canadians, the Indians were there, and I can't remember who else, maybe it was the Czechs. They came in, and they met each one of us in the room there. The Canadians, of course, were great to be around, and we were all lined up by our beds talking to them.

The North Vietnamese had us walk outside and started calling off our names. When each individual name was called, that guy went over and got in line. Once we were all lined up, the SRO hollered, "Dress right, dress. Attention!" We marched out of the Hanoi Hilton in military formation into the sunlight of freedom.

Busses idled outside, and a huge crowd was gathered out there. They were as quiet as mice. Nobody was gesturing to us. The Vietnamese had made a big deal out of telling us not to make any demonstration when we were released. In other words, don't flip off the crowd. Well, the crowd was there, and Risner had told them, "We will behave as long as you behave. If you do not behave, we will be prepared for it."

They took that very seriously. They told their people to be quiet and polite, and everyone was.

We got on the busses, small busses, and we went across the Paul Doumer bridge which was back up and being used again. They stopped short of Gia Lam airport in a kind of holding area. I assume it was where passengers assembled when they came in.

They brought out cookies and beer. It was in the morning, I don't drink in the morning, and I very seldom drink beer at all. However, that morning I had a sip and a couple of cookies.

Then we got back on the busses and headed out onto the hardstand. There were two or three C-141s out there. An American full colonel by the name of Bennett and the Rabbit were there. We all got lined up again, and the Rabbit called off our names. As each name was called, that guy would step across an imaginary line and salute Colonel Bennett. Then he would shake Bennett's hand.

Each one of us was personally escorted out to the C-141 by a crewman. They were going back and forth walking us into the airplane and to our seats. We were disoriented. We were happy, of course, we were ecstatic, but we were dazed. Shit, what do you say?

We sat down and soon the engines were started. I noticed somebody was standing up. The loadmaster said, "Everybody sit down and buckle up," but this one guy didn't. Then the loadmaster hollered, "Well, hang on to something." When we got out to the end of the runway, a couple of the guys were still standing up, and he yelled out, "Here we go. Hang on."

That was probably the first time a C-141 ever took off with everybody not seated and strapped in. When we broke ground, everybody was whooping and hollering. The aircraft commander called as we crossed the North Vietnamese coast outbound, and he said, "We are now feet wet." He meant we were over the South China Sea and officially out of North Vietnam. Everybody just went crazy.

JACK LEAVING HANOI

Chapter 20★ Ed's Dog

AS WE STARTED TO LEAVE DOGPATCH, there was a hell of a hubbub up at one of the trucks. We heard a lot of, "Bao cao, bao cao," meaning, "Attention, please." It is a polite way of calling for attention. Whenever we wanted the attention of an officer or one of the guards, we would yell, "Bao cao." There was a hell of a lot of hooraying going on up there, and the guys in my truck didn't know what the hell was happening.

A couple of months before, one of the guards in Ed Davis's building came into the courtyard carrying a little puppy. It was cute as hell, and Davis said to the guard, "Where did you get the dog?"

The guard told Ed that he had bought it from the villagers. Of course, all of this is in pidgin English and gestures, because neither one of them spoke the other's language at all. Ed was playing with the dog when it came time to eat. The guard started to leave, and then he remembered his dog.

Davis offered, "I'll watch the dog while you get the food."

"OK," replied the guard, and off he went.

He returned with the food and Davis was sitting there holding and petting the dog while we ate.

Davis said, "I'll look after the dog while you go take a nap." It was the quiet hour and the guard agreed. He knew that the dog couldn't get out of the courtyard.

That night, Davis offered to keep the dog, and the guard said fine. The guard knew that if Davis was looking after the dog in that building, there would be no damn way in the world that another guard could come along and steal it.

Now why did the guard have the dog? There was no doubt about that. The reason he bought it was to feed him and fatten him up. When Tet came, in the January or February time frame, the oriental New Year, he would kill the puppy and eat it. Dog is considered a delicacy there.

So, Davis looked after the dog. He bathed the dog. The dog slept in his building on the mat next to him, and he was a very cuddly little guy. Then time came for us to leave and go back down to Hanoi. Davis walked out with the rest of us. The building he was in also housed John Stavast. Stavast was the SRO of the camp, and the guards knew that.

Davis picked up his dog and his bedroll, and he went out and started to climb on the truck. The guard came up to him and demanded, "Give me that dog."

Davis said, "No, It's my dog now." He'd been looking after the dog for a couple months by that time. "I've been bathing the dog. I've been feeding the dog. It's my dog."

The guard brought his gun down on Davis, chambered a round and said, "Give me that dog right now."

Davis began yelling, "Bao cao, bao cao."

This, of course, gets the senior Vietnamese officer's attention, and he came back and asked what the hell was going on.

The guard tells him, "This prisoner has my dog."

Davis says, "Bullshit. It's my dog. I've been looking after that dog. He hasn't paid a bit of attention to him in two months."

The guard is upset. Davis is upset. Stavast chimes in and calmly told the officer, "Oh, by the way, none of us are going anywhere without that dog."

It was out and out blackmail. The camp commander looked at Stavast. He was so mad at John that he could bite nails. John was getting set to yell at everyone to go on a sit-down strike, and the camp commander didn't doubt that he would do it.

The camp commander turned to the guard and told him, "Look, let him carry the dog down to Hanoi. You get in the truck and carry your gun. You'll get your dog back when we get to Hanoi."

The guard was a simple farm kid, and he said okay. So, he climbed in with his rifle, Davis climbed in with the dog, and off we went to Hanoi. We stopped once or twice on the way down there. This was the night of the twentieth, and I'd won my martini.

When we were about halfway down to Hanoi, they stopped the whole procession, and we all got out to take a piss. One of our guys sidled up to a guard and asked, "Is the war over?"

The guard nodded and said, "Bombing stop, bombing stop. Go back to Paris."

We were pretty excited about it, and so we roared down to Hanoi and back into the big prison. The guys there started yelling at us that we had missed the bombings, "the biggest show on earth," and Davis had his dog.

He moved back into one of the big rooms in the Hoa Lo prison, and he started teaching the dog to bark at the guards when they walked in the door. We got there on the night of the twenty first of January. The first group wasn't going to be released until February twelfth. We were there for several weeks, and Davis's puppy was learning to bark at the guards. It was cute as hell, laughable, and it never would have happened before the bombing stopped.

Finally, the twelfth of February rolled around, and it was time to go home. Davis came ambling along, carrying his dog, and the guard was there. He knew that Davis was going off to a place he couldn't go, and he shouted, "Give me that fucking dog right now."

Davis really got upset. He yelled, "I'm not giving you this dog. I've been looking after this dog for months. It's my dog, and the dog is going with me."

The guard again put the gun right on him again, chambered in a round and he said, "Give me that dog."

I was watching this, looking out the window and across the yard. It was early in the morning, and all these guys were lined up, all the old timers, Stockdale, Risner, Denton, Davis, the damned dog, the camp commander, and the guard. Everyone is all excited.

The camp commander, the big camp commander, the head guy of the whole damn prison system came walking over then, because he was overseeing it. He demands, "What the hell is going on here?" He had no idea that Davis had this dog.

Davis explained that he has had the dog for a long time, and that it was his dog. The guard said, "No, it is my dog. I paid for it." He argued his case, and he was upset.

Then Risner walked up to check things out. He was the ranking POW officer of the whole damn shooting match, and they knew that too.

He stepped up and said, "Oh by the way, none of us are going anywhere without that dog."

Right before our eyes, the camp commander asked the guard how much he paid for the dog. The guy told him and the senior Vietnamese officer brings out his purse and gave money to the guard. So, Davis marches out of the Hanoi Hilton carrying the dog onto the C-141 and off to Clark.

We found out later that after the first group landed in the Philippines, Davis's group was on floor four and five of the Clark hospital, and that the little dog was scampering up and down the halls. The nurses were captivated. Davis had liberated a communist dog.

Then the immigration guys came in and announced to Davis that the dog was going to have to stay in quarantine for six months. "Those are our laws."

Davis looks at him and says, "That dog is leaving with me, and I'm leaving day after tomorrow."

The immigration guy went on, "Look, you blackmailed the Vietnamese, but you're back in our custody now, and you can't blackmail us."

At that Risner interjects, "By the way, none of us are leaving without that dog."

When Risner stated what he did to that Vietnamese commander, he had placed himself right between Kissinger and Tram Van Dong. That was a bad place to be for career progression. Now a short little brigadier general was standing there watching Risner threaten the immigration guy with a proclamation that nobody was going anywhere without the dog.

This general who was there to see that this sort of shit didn't happen went straightaway to a phone and called the Chief of Staff of the White House, H. R. Halderman. The general related what was going on to him.

Halderman then went in and told the tale to Richard Nixon. The President of the United States growled, "You tell them to bring that damn dog right now." He told them that Davis was taking the dog with him, and Davis did.

So, back to the United States went Davis carrying his dog.

Later came the April White House dinner with all three hundred and fifty POWs there. In all there were some thirty-five hundred people there including wives, sweethearts, family and friends.

After it was over, Nixon was showing us through the White House. He was up ahead of me somewhere, and I heard him say something like, "Where is Ed Davis, by the way?"

Everyone started to yell, "Davis, Davis, the boss wants to talk to you." Davis came through the crowd in his mess dress and said, "Yes sir?"

The President gave him an amused scowl and asked, "Davis, where's your dog?"

"Mr. President, I thought it would be a good idea if I left the dog home tonight."

Nixon looked at him, "Davis you have no idea how you have enhanced your Naval career with that decision."

Chapter 21 ★ Clark Air Base

WHEN WE LANDED AT CLARK, IT was just about dark. We taxied in, and after they shut the engines down, I could hear this chant, a really loud chant. I didn't know what it was. Soon we discovered that there were thousands of people out there chanting "well - come - home, well - come - home."

The doors opened, and they started calling out each one of us individually by our rank and name. We walked out and started down the boarding ramp. The ramp had some spring in it, and I was almost flipped off it.

We were met by our ambassador to the Philippines and the CINCPAC (Commander in Chief, Pacific), Admiral Gaylor. We saluted, shook hands, got in a bus, and off we went to the hospital. This was really a terrifically moving moment for me.

We got up to the hospital, and they assigned us to rooms. The medical folks knew about Red McDaniel and the torture he had suffered. They were very concerned about that. The first group out had brought word that Red was going to be in the second group, and that I knew a good bit about his situation. They put us together in a hospital room where I could help with the debriefing of the doctors.

The doctors came in very soon after we arrived. There was a neurologist there, a heart guy, and a whole bunch of other medical experts, the whole nine yards. We had the best that the Air Force and the Navy had available there at Clark AFB to look after us.

They spent about an hour with Red and me, debriefing us about what he had gone through. The neurologist was all over him. The cardiologist there really checked him out very carefully, very quickly. It was obvious that Red had a lot of nerve damage. He had a lot of scars, just as I do, but they decided he was not in any immediate danger.

When we got to Clark AB, I was a little taken aback by how well the senior Air Force representative there understood our system with the SRO and the way we were organized. He seemed to grasp the way we were set up. He turned to Colonel Gaddis, and he said, "Norm, I want you to tell your men not to leave the hospital."

I thought, "What the hell are you talking about? I haven't gone from one slammer to another, have I?"

Norm said, "Well, let me think about that for a minute."

"It is really important. We want to guarantee your safety," he explained.

I said, "Colonel Gaddis, sir, I've been dreaming for years about going to the Clark Air Force Base Officers' Club and having a couple of drinks. I mean, this is ridiculous not to be able to go over there."

The guy just about had a heart attack. He said, "We just cannot have you wandering around the base. Please."

Norm thought about it for a while and finally he spoke, "OK, no one will leave the hospital unless they are escorted."

Well, I was really taken back. I mean we all shut up and said yes sir, because that was the way our system worked. There was no arguing with him. He said that's the way it's going to be, and that's the way it was.

But I was surprised that the guy was that astute about how our system worked. I mentioned it to one of the nurses.

She said, "Well, he's a fast learner."

The story I heard later was that when the first group of pows came out, this senior guy didn't talk to the SRO. The first night the first group was in the hospital he simply gave an order, "None of you are to leave the hospital."

The second night they took them to the BX. When they got there, three girls were standing outside the BX. The three were airline stews, and one of them handed Spike Nasmyth a note. The note read, "I want to be first."

Spike read the note, looked at her and said, "I'll be going out the back door, where it says Fire Exit."

She told him, "We'll be back there."

Spike went right out the back door, and these three gals were out there as advertised. They all jumped into a car, drove off, and had an all-night party.

Well, the next morning this same colonel, who later asked Norm to tell us not to leave, was wandering around, and he finds out he's short one POW. He sees his whole career flashing before his eyes. He can't believe it. About that time, Spike came walking in the door wearing his pajamas, his pajama coat, and slippers.

The colonel came running up to him and said, "Where in the hell have you been?"

"Where in the hell do you think I've been?"

The colonel spouted, "I ordered you not to leave the hospital."

Spike told him, "You're not my SRO. The SRO didn't tell me a damned thing. I don't work for you," and walked on past him.

The guy got smart, really quick. Somebody told him that if the SRO told us not to leave, we wouldn't leave. Sure enough, in our group none of us stirred out of that hospital. It was interesting and very frustrating.

We were on the fourth and fifth floors of the Clark Air Base hospital. One night, I decided to go down in the elevator to get something to eat. I noticed that there were senior sergeants at every door, always very polite, "Can I help you sir?"

This was three o'clock in the morning. I was going down in an elevator and a chief master sergeant was driving the elevator. I said, "OK, Chief, I've been gone a long time, but I know our unit manning hasn't changed to the point that we have chief master sergeants running elevators. What the hell is going on here?"

He replied, "You are absolutely right. We are all volunteers. All the NCOs you see here in the hospital are volunteers. There were thousands of us who volunteered, and somewhere between fifty to seventy-five were chosen. I'm so honored to be here. I can't believe it."

The memory of that almost makes me cry.

They had a dietitian there for the first group. They had baby food, Pablum and all that kind of crap, and the guys said, "Get all that shit out of here. We're eating regular food." Leroy Stutz sat down and proceeded to eat thirteen eggs right off the reel. Then he came back and ate twelve more. There was nothing wrong with our appetites. We were able to adjust to the food very quickly. That part of it was just like we had never been gone.

We thought the food was great. The hospital staff didn't necessarily agree with that, but they did everything they could to make it pleasant. We had steaks everywhere and ice cream and all. It was pretty neat.

Then the phone calls started. I was apprehensive about getting on the phone with my wife, because I had no idea what to expect. I had told Charlie Plumb that I thought it would go very smoothly, just fine.

He said, "Jack, we've been gone a long, long time. There are going to be a lot of problems." He was very prophetic.

We were at Clark for thirty-six hours when I got on the phone with Verna. She was very polite, very nice. She sounded sort of warm, and she said she was looking forward to seeing me. She told me that the boys were fine, and they would see me at March Air Force Base, because that's where I was scheduled to come in.

I said, "Okay great," and I hung up. I called her again and this time she seemed to warm up a little bit more. I got more assurance that things were going to be alright.

By the way, when we got to Clark, we had those names of the twenty-three people we had found just before we left, and we gave them to that little general who was there.

He called Kissinger right away, and Kissinger called Phan Van Dong. Kissinger said, "I know you've got them, and I know where they are. I'm sending a plane to get them."

Those twenty-three folks were at Clark for twelve of the thirty-six hours that I was there. That's how fast Henry got them out of there. Ted Guy told me, "You saved my life."

I said, "I didn't save your life. The guy who whistled saved your life."

We never knew what the hell the Vietnamese were going to do. We had no idea what they were up to, and we simply didn't have those names. We had Ted Guy's name, but we didn't have the other twenty-two at all, and Henry Kissinger didn't have them either.

I've written about that story. When they had the Senate Select Committee on POW/MIA Affairs in the early 90s, I sent those facts to Senator Smith in writing. I got a form letter back saying thank you for your interest and that kind of bullshit.

I've been asked whether or not anyone was left behind. That is the question we get asked the most. Did we leave anybody behind? I think that you will find that most returned POWs will say that those Americans who were shot down over North Vietnam, and captured by the Vietnamese, either died in prison or were returned. I think that is our general consensus, though I have begun to have some doubts in my heart.

About those shot down in Laos, Cambodia and South Vietnam, we have no idea whatsoever. The story about finding Floyd Thompson is certainly typical of what I'm talking about.

We had absolutely no idea that Floyd was there. He was there longer than any of us. He was there longer than Ev Alverez. Floyd died a while back down in Key West, a very lonely, broken and unhappy man who had a hell of a lot of trouble after he got out of jail. They kept working with him and promoted him to full colonel, but he went through several wives, and he was a desperate alcoholic when he died. That was very, very sad. He died prematurely in his late sixties.

We got fitted for uniforms, and the docs checked us over, and then the dentist came in. He looked in my mouth and said, "Oh man."

I asked, "That bad, Doc?"

"It's worse than that."

I said, "Can you fix it?"

"I'm not sure," he mumbled.

I thought, "Damn, that's bad."

I was there at March Air Force Base in California for sixteen days. I spent three to four hours of every day in the dentist's chair at March. When I left there, I damn near had a suntan from the lamp over the chair. They did more work on me in those sixteen days than most people have done in a lifetime. They did root canals. They did bridgework. They did an incredible job of saving my teeth.

Today, more than thirty years later, the dentists have had to replace a good bit of the work that was done, but it lasted for over twenty-five years. They did a hell of a job, and I'll never forget that.

One time, the doc came in and he asked, "Is there anything I can get you?"

I said, "Since they won't let me go to the Officers' club. I want a scotch and soda."

He took out a prescription pad and started to write out a prescription for a scotch and soda.

I said, "Doc, forget that. I'm not going to have you write that out."

The doctors looked at my knee, injured when I landed for the first time in North Vietnam. They messed around with it, and finally the orthopedic guys declared that it had healed itself. They said that eventually I might have to have arthroscopic surgery on it. What they were really saying was that if you live long enough that might be the case, and sure enough, I did. I eventually had surgery on my left knee. They took out a bunch of old cartilage, and it's as good as new now.

At Clark AB, we had escort officers. They were chosen from among our very closest friends. My hospital room door opened and in walked Charley Hartman. He is one of the closest friends I have in the world. He had volunteered to come out and bring me home.

Each one of us had an escort officer who was a very close friend. Red Wilson was escorted by Darrell "Big D" Simmons from Luke Air Force Base. It was quite a rendezvous, because we knew almost all these guys, the Air Force escort officers. The Navy guys knew their escort officers, too. On the C-141 to Hawaii, we had thirty to forty POWs and the same number of escort officers. We all had assigned bunks if we wanted to use them, and the escort officers were just jumping to take care of us.

Chapter 22★ Honolulu and Beyond

WE TOOK OFF FROM CLARK AIR BASE in the Philippines and flew to Hawaii. We were scheduled to arrive there at three o'clock in the morning.

They told us that we could only have one guest at a time coming in to visit us during our stay there.

My friend, Gene "Charlie" Hartman lived in Hawaii at the time. I told him that I wanted his wife, Joan to come with him when he came to visit. He told me about the one visitor rule, but I said, "Ah, come on, they aren't going to be that strict about it."

He told me that they said they were.

I just said, "I want her in here," and she was. She stood right there the whole time. She was a great friend of mine and is to this day. They are both alive and well in Washington, D.C.

They told me that I had more visitors than Risner did. I found that hard to believe, but I knew a lot of people who were stationed there at PACAF Headquarters. Somewhere around one hundred and thirty people came in to see me while I was there. Major General Boots Blesse was one of those who came. It was a hell of a deal and quite a terrific homecoming.

Next, we took off and went on to Travis AFB in Northern California. When we landed, there was another huge crowd to greet us. Some of us were loaded onto a smaller airplane, and we flew on down to March AFB, near Riverside, California. I was having a lot of trouble keeping from crying. I mean I was really emotional about all of this.

Dick Stratton told me, "Just smile. If you smile, you can't cry." It's amazing but it was true. If you're smiling, you can't cry. I thought, well OK, I've learned something new there.

We landed at March AFB, and my mother and father, my brother, my wife, Verna, and my three boys had all come to greet me. Of course, my littlest boy didn't remember me from a load of coal. He was about 16 months old when I last saw him, and now six years had passed.

It was a nice reunion, but I noticed right off that Verna seemed a little reserved and withdrawn. We were taken to the hospital, and I was given a room there. I asked if I had to stay in it, and they told me that I didn't. It was there if I wanted to use it while I was at March. Verna had been given a room in the VOQ (Visiting Officers' Quarters).

I said, "I'll go with her."

When we got to the room there was certainly tension there. We had been given no advice on how to act. We had been given no counseling of any sort, no marriage counseling or anything else. There was nobody to tell us to take it slow, take it easy, get to know one another. None of that happened, and I've often regretted that it didn't. I'm not sure if it would have made any difference, though.

We finally got back to the VOQ, and we sat up and talked for two or three hours. If I'd had the brains that God gave a goose, I would have gone back to the hospital. We slept together that night, and we did OK, I guess. She was trying hard, but it was obvious that there was something missing.

One of the first things that impacted me very soon after I got there occurred when we went to the officers' club for dinner one evening. That was in the days of acid rock, and I had never heard such music. It was so loud. I could barely stand it. I have never been able to be around loud people and loud noises. It was just unbelievable to me how earsplitting it was. It was a very difficult and uncomfortable experience for me.

Verna traveled back and forth between Tucson and March, but I had to stay there because of my teeth. My boys went back to Tucson, and I remained there for sixteen days. Eventually they put me back together again. When the dentist came out to finish up that last day, I was handed my dental record. It was a standard sized 8.5" by 11" page, and it was three quarters filled in. Of course, I felt a lot better. The VA has been looking after me ever since.

Eventually, the Air Force assigned us another airplane, and we were hauled off to Tucson, Arizona. Among the thousands of people there to meet us were the mayor of Tucson, the president of the University of Arizona, and the Commander of the 355th

Tactical Fighter Wing, Col. Fred Haeffner. Bands were there playing, and it was overwhelming. Fred Haeffner was a lifelong friend. I loved him and am so sorry he died prematurely.

When I stepped off that airplane as a Lieutenant Colonel, Fred looked at me, gestured around, and said, "I have 72 A-7s here just waiting for you to fly them." He really treated me wonderfully.

TUCSON WELCOME HOME

JACK'S SON, STEVEN, WEARING A BUTTON THAT HE MADE WHEN THE FAMILY LEARNED JACK WAS ALIVE AND A POW

Chapter 23★ Questions

THEN THE QUESTIONS STARTED. The press was right there, and they felt that they deserved answers. They wanted to know how we were treated. It had become apparent, from the time the first group of POWs came home, and then the second, that we were not going to answer all their questions. This drove the press crazy.

The leadership of the 4th Allied POW Wing had decided that nobody would answer any questions concerning treatment of POWs until the entire group was released. They were worried that if we started to tell the truth, the Vietnamese would stop releasing people. That was very smart on the part of General Flynn, Colonel Risner, Admiral Stockdale, Admiral Denton and the rest of our leaders.

We clammed up, and the press couldn't stand it. We just weren't talking. Eventually we were cleared to talk, and when we started to tell our story, it shocked the American public. I found it very difficult to talk about how we were treated to audiences. I've had some people tell me that I did a great job of it, and others say that it was hard for them to relate to what I told them.

How many people do you know who have ever even spent the night in jail? It is very hard for people to relate to being in physical and mental isolation, solitary confinement, and being subjected to actual torture.

Americans don't understand what that sort of treatment means. We had been locked away, twelve thousand miles away from home for years. We had been intimidated and tortured, physically and psychologically. I worked very hard trying to explain what that meant and how it affected us.

We were asked about homosexual behavior. I can tell you in all the time that I was there I never heard of a single homosexual occurrence. I was asked, "Did anybody get laid up there?"

My answer was always, "Not to the best of my knowledge." The only time I ever heard of anything approaching that was when Fred Cherry told us that one time a Vietnamese girl had climbed on top of him, and he was trying to get her to stop, because he was afraid someone would walk in the door and catch them.

The toughest group I ever had to brief consisted of my superior officers. They had no inhibitions, and it was hard to get information across. How was the food, how was the weather, what were the Vietnamese like? These questions were asked thousands of times.

The question I was asked that won the prize, topped off everything, occurred at the Corvallis Country Club at a reception for me in May of 1973. My brother was standing by my side. There were over seven hundred people there in a room that was designed for about three hundred. It was absolutely packed. It was very noisy, and I was having a hard time containing myself with that much pressure.

A woman appeared right in front of me. She was the wife of the dean of the school of business, a good friend of mine. She said out of the clear blue sky, "Jack, how much golf did you play while you were in Hanoi."

I almost said to her, "Lady, you gotta be shitting me," but I didn't. I was shocked that anyone would ask me that.

I said, "Ma'am, I'm afraid you misunderstood how we were treated."

I turned to my brother and said, "We're leaving."

He was white as a sheet and said, "Roger that." We left the reception held in my honor. I was shocked that anybody would ask me that question. We went up to the house, and I got a bit drunk.

Later, I attended another reception at the Tucson Country Club. I was asked by Dick Gerhart, a great friend of mine, to go out there for a dinner dance. He told me that the dumbest guy in the world is going to be there. He owned a Cadillac/Oldsmobile dealership in town.

About ten o'clock in the evening, this car dealer comes up, and he had been behaving all right, drinking iced tea. Out a clear blue sky he asked, "Jack, did you play golf when you were in Hanoi?" I looked at Gerhart, and he looked at me.

He said, "I told you." He didn't actually say it, he mouthed it.

I told him, "I didn't play, I caddied."

"You caddied?"

I said, "Yeah, once a year they had the Hanoi open, and I always got to caddy for Ho Chi Minh. He always won, and I got a great tip."

This guy stood up and at the top of his lungs, he yells to this crowd of several hundred people, "Guys, Jack caddied for Ho Chi Minh."

Chapter 24 ★ B-52s and POWs

THE BOMBING OF HANOI BY THE B-52s in Linebacker unquestionably shortened the war. The best book on that subject is, *The Eleven Days of Christmas*. I strongly recommend it.

The book points out what Richard Nixon told me and several others who were standing around his pool in San Clemente when we went out there one time. Nixon said, "I told Moyer," referring to the chairman of the Joint Chiefs, "that either he did it right, or I was going to come over there and do it for him."

I think that is also in his book, *Nixon*. What he meant was that "I want to terrify those people." He was not really interested in military targets. He wanted to scare the crap out of them. He wanted to drive them back to Paris and sign the peace agreements.

On the 26th of February, we were supposed to be released, but we weren't. Somewhere in there, on the 2nd or 3rd of March, while I was busy trying to get names, Jim Kasler and I were out walking in the yard. One of the young North Vietnamese officers came up to me and said, "Be, you think B-52 come back if you not release soon?"

I looked at him and said very slowly, "I do not think B-52 come back, I know B-52 come back."

He looked at me, and his eyes got really wide. He said, "I think Nixon crazy."

I looked him in the eye and told him, "President Nixon is not crazy, he is insane, and he hates your guts."

With that he ran off yelling at the top of his voice that he had gotten some more intelligence from the Yankee Air Pirates.

That is what Nixon wanted to do. He wanted to make them think that he had lost his mind. If you read his book that comes out, though you have to read between the lines.

The fact that we had to lose fifteen B-52s was tragic. This is particularly true because SAC couldn't get their shit together and had their bombers coming in on a stream, flying the same altitudes and headings night after night, rather than varying them. This was suicidal for those crews.

The issue of the MIAs and POWs concerned me so much that I got hold of a woman who used to work for me and was now in intelligence, in the DIA. By the time she got back to me, she was a colonel, and I was out of the Air Force.

I had expressed my concerns to her about leaving people behind. She had done a paper on it which was declassified. Then she told me that her boss, who was a Lt. General at the time, told her that I was free to come to Washington, and he would show me everything they had.

I told her that I remembered that in April of 1973, the *Tucson Daily Citizen* carried a press release from the North Vietnamese foreign ministry which said that the Laotians had told them that they had executed around three hundred Americans, because they couldn't keep them. I was absolutely stunned when I saw that number. I told her, "I can't find that anywhere."

I know that I didn't imagine reading it. It should have caused a huge uproar in the nation, but it didn't. She went back and looked. Sure enough, she found that also. So, whether the North Vietnamese were covering up what happened in Laos, or helping the Laotians do it by saying that, I don't know, but that's one thing I remember.

One of our number who has been very heavily involved in the POW/MIA issue is my good friend Red McDaniel. His full name is Eugene Barker McDaniel. Red has, in the opinion of some, all but gone over the edge on this MIA issue, but I choose to say that he was just very dedicated in his pursuit of it.

The situation has evolved to the point that some of the guys are really not comfortable being around Red, because he has become sort of an evangelist on the subject. Maybe he's right. I don't know. He wrote a pretty good book that included a piece I wrote called "Before Honor."

That's what I know about the MIA issue. We searched, to the extent we could, all over North Vietnam for people who were missing. I looked for Jim Magnuson as a matter of fact. Jim had been shot down in 1965 flying an F-105, and I never saw a trace of him. You can't know for sure, but could they have kept people away from us? You bet your boots they could have and likely did.

The occasion on which I found those twenty-three guys just before we were released is a disconcerting event. We didn't know about any of them before, and that is disturbing to me. We had always been alert to the possibility of others, but we never found anybody else. That was just a fluke and a lucky one. I think if they had not been discovered, they might never have come home.

Pete Peterson, our ambassador to Vietnam in 1998, talked to a group of us when we went to Hanoi that year. He said, "We haven't found anyone. We haven't found evidence of anyone that the North Vietnamese have kept against their will."

Pete was as sincere and as honest as he could possibly be, but I'm not sure he is right. The situation with the Laotians, the Cambodians, and the Viet Cong is a whole different issue.

Let me say another word or two about Ho Chi Minh. I went over there knowing a good bit about him. I discovered that they had done a marvelous job of reeducating their people. I never met an English speaker who had the slightest idea that Ho had spent thirty-two years outside of Vietnam. None of them knew that.

Most of the Vietnamese thought that Ho had been working in Vietnam all those years to make things better, but that just wasn't the case. He had been gone for most of that time.

One true thing about Ho is that, like Marshall Tito of Yugoslavia, he became a benevolent dictator. The people truly loved him, even though by the most conservative estimate, he killed at least one hundred thousand of his people who did not want to go along with the program of living on the collective farms.

He slaughtered a great many of his fellow countrymen, but despite that, he was loved and respected. When he died, they had a funeral dirge that went on for days and days. I regretted so much that we had not cultivated him in the same way we did Marshal Tito.

We unquestionably cultivated Tito. Those guys were over there flying F-84s that we gave them. Ho appealed to us to do the same thing for him and he was turned down flat because of the French. I've often regretted that. I wasn't interested in the United States climbing in bed with the Communists, but once I got over there, I discovered that Vietnamese Communism was actually about seventy-five percent nationalistic.

There is one more thing about the bombing in 1972. When we got back, one of Ross Perot's guys, who was on his staff, and who had a Doctorate in International Relations met with us. I think it was at Maxwell AFB. He was asked about his relationship with the North Vietnamese.

Throughout the war, when the North Vietnamese wanted to get the straight answer on a subject, they would call this man up and ask him to come to Vientiane, Laos. He would tell the State Department that the North Vietnamese had called him, and that he was going to Vientiane. He would brief the State Department on his discussions when he got back.

The bombing of North Vietnam by the B-52s started, and he got a call in Dallas. They told him that they had to talk to him immediately. The said that they were an "unofficial" delegation of North Vietnam. Well, there is no such thing as an unofficial delegation from Hanoi. They asked if he would please come to Vientiane by the most direct means available, and he did.

He got over there, went into a room, and there was none of the usual palaver. They said, "We have a question that we want to ask you, and we have to have an answer within twenty-four hours." He agreed.

They asked, "Under your system of jurisprudence your courts, how long would it take for the American public, through your courts, to force President Nixon to stop the bombing of North Vietnam."

He told them, "You just gave me a PHD thesis topic that might take me two years to research."

They said, "We HAVE to have your answer as best you can give us in twenty-four hours."

He said, "Then you're going to get a twenty-four-hour answer."

Later when he came back to them, he said, "This is the best I can do. I've been on the phone constantly talking to scholars and experts. Assuming that the American people want to do that, they possibly could force President Nixon to stop the bombing in about eighteen months through our courts."

That was translated to them, and one of them said, with anger, "Eighteen months? We can't take this for eighteen more days."

That word was carried back to Hanoi. When you read the book *The Eleven Days of Christmas*, the night of the 26th was decisive. On that night the attack came at Hanoi from all different directions, and they overwhelmed the defenses. The North Vietnamese realized that they couldn't handle that. That in conjunction with the reported eighteen-month time frame resulted in them, saying "That's it." They threw in the towel and went back to Paris.

Chapter 25★ Thoughts and Impressions

AS I REVIEW MY COMMENTARY about going to Air Command and Staff College, then on to Davis Monthan, and finally over to Ubon, I realize I really hadn't said a single thing about my impressions of the war in Vietnam. During the time, I was at Command and Staff, in F-4 training, and when I was at Ubon, I developed some opinions I think could be useful in understanding my experience and the conclusions I reached.

I remember Chappie James getting up on the stage at Davis Monthan at an aircrew meeting with students, both front and back seaters. He said something like, "You know, this war is a shitty war, but it's the only war we have, and it's better than nothing."

I thought that here is a guy who must have lost his mind, because nobody in their right mind is out looking for a war.

Then I remembered reading an article about Harrison Salisbury, a reporter with the New York Times who went to Hanoi and reported from there. He was criticized rather sharply at the time for some of the things he said that sounded pro-North Vietnamese. In fact, as he pointed out when he came home, it was very difficult for him to send out anything meaningful for the simple reason that he was being so closely watched and his stories monitored by the North Vietnamese.

And now, as one who has been there, I can certainly empathize with that point of view better than I could at the time. Before I was shot down, I saw my great friend Dick Stratton in a photo in Life Magazine, and it was scary. You remember that Stratton was pictured bowing from the waist and turning to face all four directions. It was theorized that we were probably being treated in North Vietnam like Pavlov's dogs and being conditioned in our behavior.

That was certainly not true. Stratton was a super gutsy guy. When I first saw the videos of him, I thought God Almighty, what in the world have they done to this guy. The level of pressure and abuse he had suffered and was receiving, was beyond my comprehension at the time. The fact that I was going to experience the same treatment soon, never dawned on me. The courage and ingenuity he demonstrated in order to pass information to the world was extraordinary, displaying the very best of our warriors.

I spent a good bit of time reading about Ho Chi Minh. I was also interested in the rules of war. The Navy and Marine Corps had eight or nine of them, the Army around ten, and the Air Force ten or eleven. The most important, though unwritten, rule of war for every service is, or should be, know thine enemy.

I discovered that Ho Chi Minh had been out of the country for a good part of his life. He left Vietnam in 1913, and he spent the next thirty-one years outside the country. He came back to Vietnam around 1944, crossing the border while evading capture by the French and the Japanese. It actually was the Vichy French. The Japanese were occupying Vietnam at the time.

He spent the earlier portion of Second World War in Moscow. Ho traveled throughout the world and worked as a cook in Chicago and a longshoreman in New York. He spent a great deal of time in Paris and became fluent in French. If you wanted to get along in Vietnam when the French occupied it, you had to be able to speak French, and many of the Vietnamese I met did speak French.

As a matter of fact, Charley Southwick, my long-time cellmate, was asked when he was first captured, "Parley vous Francais?"

Charley looked at the interrogator and said, "No."

And they just beat the shit out of him, screaming, "You lie, you lie."

He told them that everybody knows parley vous Francais means do you speak French. He did his damn best to tell them that "Habla Espanol, Spreken ze Deutch, and Parley vous Francais" are phrases known everywhere.

That didn't make any difference to the Vietnamese. They just pounded the hell out of him. I laugh about it now and thought it was a funny story. It would never have dawned on me to ask, "What do you mean," if they asked me that. I would have said the same thing Charley did and gotten beaten up for it.

As I said before, I spent a good bit of time studying Ho Chi Minh, and I had the initial impression that Ho was probably about seventy-five percent communist and twenty-five percent nationalist. When I got over there, I found it to be the exact opposite. I now believe that he was seventy-five percent nationalist and twenty-five percent communist.

Ho was a Vietnamese nationalist first and always, and he was a damned good politician as well. He was also an extremely formidable adversary. The people in Vietnam truly loved him. That was obvious. I spent a good bit of time learning what happened in the aftermath of the French defeat at Dien Bien Phu, when the French, the Americans, the Chinese, and the Russians went to Geneva to hold the Indochinese Peace Conference.

That was the famous peace conference where John Foster Dulles had the opportunity to shake Chou En-Lai's hand and declined, thereby shutting down Sino-American relations for twenty-one years. Regardless, Ho was at that conference also, pleading for an independent Vietnam. All he ended up with was a somewhat independent Vietnam above the 17th parallel, but he was obliged to go underground not too long thereafter, because the French and the Americans were after him.

At that peace conference, they decided that two years in the future there would be independent elections in Vietnam. However, when the two years passed and the election time came up, the Americans chose not to honor their promise to hold them for the simple reason that had there been elections, Ho would have won hands down.

There is no question about it. He would have won in the South, and he would have won in the North. John Foster Dulles decided not to let the elections proceed although that was the promise made at the Geneva Accords on the ending of the war on Indochina. Instead, he appointed the Diem family and Diem himself to rule South Vietnam.

When you look at that whole thing, it was a very sad situation. What we were really saying was, "If you don't agree with us, we aren't going to let you gain political power." One would hope someday we would get smart enough to realize that deciding what we believe other peoples should do, and how they should live, is not necessarily the wisest course of action. The question is whether they know enough about their region and situation to be able to do what's right for themselves.

I'm not saying that Ho Chi Minh was the best answer, but it is useful to remember that when you read the Vietnamese Declaration of Independence, it is an absolute copy of ours. What he was attempting to do, and this was totally missed or ignored by John Foster Dulles, was to gain independence for his country and to be treated much as the United States treated Yugoslavia. I found all of that to be very interesting.

I had a great deal of trouble with the domino theory. The Vietnamese didn't have any significant history of running off across borders. I had a great deal of trouble understanding how it was in our vital national interest to be fighting over there. I couldn't find evidence that there was a single solitary mineral, rare gem source like diamonds or anything of a natural product nature, that was significant enough to our vital national interest to fight a war over. There were no raw materials, no oil, or anything else we needed from there, yet we declared it to be in our vital national interest to fight over control of it. Vital to me means life or death. I had a hell of a lot of trouble with that. I kept searching for why we were fighting in Vietnam. The more that I looked the less I found.

It bothered me that Lyndon Johnson was talking about the domino theory and our vital national interest. Yet he had no understanding of the enemy he was fighting whatsoever. Johnson said about Ho, "I am not about to be blackmailed by a yellow pigmy in black pajamas carrying a pocketknife."

My blood ran absolutely cold when I heard he had said that. I told myself, "That son of a bitch doesn't know anything about the enemy we're fighting over there." Yet, he was trying to have his guns and butter, the whole thing simultaneously.

And at the same time, he was totally micro-controlling the war from the White House including the individual JCS lists of bombing targets. If a target was on the JCS list that meant it had been personally selected by Lyndon Johnson and Bob

McNamara in the White House. That was just absolutely absurd, the total centralization of the war in the White House was just as crazy as hell.

I felt sure before I ever went over there, and it became even more obvious once I was in the theatre, that Lyndon Johnson knew absolutely nothing about Ho Chi Minh or the North Vietnamese. We didn't have anybody in charge that did. There was nobody over there like Stanley Karnow, who wrote the book, *Vietnam, A History*, or David Halberstam. Lyndon Johnson in an attempt to impress academia at Princeton, Yale, and other Ivy League schools, touted Herman Kahn's theory of escalation which in essence said, "Don't worry about what you lost today, worry about what you're going to lose tomorrow."

There was only one small problem. Ho Chi Minh never read Kahn's book. He didn't understand what Johnson was trying to do, and Johnson didn't understand Ho. So, we had the blind fighting the blind.

I knew that when I observed that we weren't attacking their airfields or their ports. My great friend Lonny Ferguson was the only man I know who got an Article 15 and was later promoted to Brigadier General. He and his guys, flying F-105s, attacked a Russian freighter in Haiphong Harbor. They shot the shit out of it. Jack Broughton was the DO there at Korat, and when he got his hands on the gun camera film, he destroyed it.

Chuck Yeager was the head of the investigating team trying to figure out how to handle it. They found Broughton guilty of destroying government property. It was the biggest joke in the world. But the truth of the matter was that Lonny Ferguson went up there, the freighter fired on him, and he turned around and shot the crap out of it.

Kosygin came to Washington, and he told Johnson that we were attacking his freighters in Haiphong Harbor, and that it had to stop. Johnson replied that we were not doing any such thing. At that point Kosygin said, "I have the shell casings right here in my briefcase." At that, Johnson realized that he was probably getting his bluff called. He sent Three-Finger Jack Ryan, who was the PACAF Commander in there.

Ryan hot-boxed the crews, and finally, they fessed up. Yeah, they had shot up that freighter, but the freighter was shooting at them first.

I thought, this is crazy. We're in a war, yet the British kept supplying our enemy with stuff, though most of what the British were bringing in there was not war material. It wasn't ammunition or other weapons, but textiles, food and non-war supplies were being delivered to the North Vietnamese. The British have always prided themselves on having a foreign policy based on free trade, and that's fine, but you pay your dollar (or pound) and take your chances. But if you do ship, if you put a freighter in there in a time of war, the damned thing should be sunk.

Haiphong Harbor was still open, and I couldn't understand it. I couldn't believe what I saw when I got over there and had heard even before that. We were letting all of this material be shipped in to use against us, directly or indirectly, and we were not attacking them. The fact that it went on as long as it did is an absolute crime in my opinion. I get sick every time I think about it.

I got shot down by an airplane that never in the world should have been there. We had 58,000 kids killed. We spent untold billions of dollars in national treasure, and what did we get out of it? Nothing of value.

The Vietnam War was the second greatest disaster in history of our country, the Civil War being the first. I'll tell you right now, you can go west of the Mississippi and make the case for the Vietnam War being the single greatest disaster that ever befell this country. I'm sorry as hell it ever happened. I'll never forgive Lyndon Johnson and Robert McNamara for not listening to rational voices and to keep going with it. Worse yet, once they decided to start the bombing program, they did it half-heartedly, costing us dearly.

I'm a dyed-in-the-wool Republican, a Goldwater conservative, I really am. I know that Barry Goldwater scared the hell out of people when he said he was going to run for President. He told everyone, "I'm going to go over there, and I'm going to blow them away. I'm going to end it."

That's what he said to us at the Luke Air Force Base Officers' Club on more than one occasion when he came out there and had a drink with us. He was going to end it.

Johnson got in there and fucked around with it and was never serious about winning it. Finally, it took Dick Nixon to come in and make something happen. He told me personally, standing there with several other guys, that the biggest mistake he made as President was not going after them in 1969, like he did in December of 1972. Maybe he was correct.

I'll tell you this. Ho Chi Minh did not understand the theory of escalation. To him it was an indication of weakness. He and all of his senior officers were totally contemptuous of Lyndon Johnson. Had Johnson gone after them hammer and tongs from the onset, the war never would have gone that far. Dean Rusk and I developed a little pen pal relationship when I was at the National War College that continued for several years. Secretary Rusk and I talked about it, and of course, he was trapped right in the middle of it. It was a very bad scene. We were so poorly led, that it was just unbelievable.

Those are my impressions, and what I saw when I got there. Everybody was confused. There were no goals or national purpose stated. None of our countrymen understood what we were trying to do, and of course, we didn't understand either. All we knew was that we weren't being allowed to go after the lucrative targets. That was insane and a fatal blow to morale. The whole damned thing was a tragedy, and I was right in the middle of it.

The war was used by people for different purposes. Robin Olds had an overwhelming desire to become an ace. He wanted to shoot down five MiGs, nothing else. He was an ace in WW II, he missed Korea, but he wanted to become an ace in Vietnam. I think he ended up with four MiGs. Robin Olds was an exceptionally gifted fighter pilot, there's no question about it. But he was interested in only one thing, and that was to get up there and shoot MiGs. That was his sole focus.

That was clearly illustrated when we were finally cleared to attack one of the Vietnamese airfields. General McConnell, the Chief of Staff of the Air Force, was there at Ubon at the time.

When the order came to go after the Kep Airfield, he told Robin, "You may not lead this mission." He told him that loud and clear. "You may not lead this mission."

Then McConnell left to go wherever he was going. Colonel Olds drove him out to his T-39, saw him aboard, then came back in and took somebody's name off the board. He put his name in the flight, flying number three, and said, "He told me I couldn't lead. He didn't say I couldn't fly." Olds was the first one off the friggen runway. The only thing he was interested in was shooting MiGs.

Some people were interested in getting medals, and other guys were interested in getting promoted. There weren't too many people interested in fighting the war, because I think they became discouraged about the whole thing. That was what I observed while I was there.

POSTSCRIPT

Life went on and things evolved to a state closer to normal after I came home. I was promoted to full colonel and held several interesting and satisfying jobs in the Air Force. I was the DO of 9th Air Force at one point and was a Wing Commander, one of the most demanding and satisfying positions that an officer can hold, at another.

However, the thrust of this story is that of my experiences in captivity and the factors leading up to that condition. The events that followed don't really fit into that story and will have to wait for another telling in the recounting of my life.

I wanted to relate my experiences in prison and those of the men with whom I shared them. They are a close and loyal band of brothers. I cherish the company of those still here and the memories of those gone on. To them all, I lift a glass of cheer and remembrance.

JACK'S SILVER STAR CITATION

Silver Star
AWARDED FOR ACTIONS DURING THE VIETNAM WAR
Service: Air Force
Division: Prisoner of War (North Vietnam)
GENERAL ORDERS:
CITATION:

The President of the United States of America, authorized by Act of Congress, July 8, 1918 (amended by act of July 25, 1963), takes pleasure in presenting the Silver Star to Lieutenant Colonel Jack Linwood Van Loan, United States Air Force, for gallantry and intrepidity in action in connection with military operations against an opposing armed force during May 1967, while a Prisoner of War in North Vietnam. Ignoring international agreements on treatment of prisoners of war, the enemy resorted to mental and physical cruelties to obtain information, confessions, and propaganda materials. Lieutenant Colonel Van Loan resisted their demands by calling upon his deepest inner strengths in a manner which reflected his devotion to duty and great credit upon himself and the United States Air Force.

Statue of Jack standing in front of a mockup of his Hanoi Hilton prison. (Five Points, Columbia, South Carolina. Photo courtesy of Ron Hagell)

EPILOGUE

Reflections by Glenn Van Loan

In many ways, my life, and the lives of my two brothers have been shaped and defined by the six years our dad spent surviving in North Vietnam. Whenever I am asked the question "where are you from," my answer has always begun with "well, I grew up an Air Force brat," to indicate that I have lived many places. Families of service members generally live a different sort of life, with a heightened sense of the sacrifice involved for family members and, more so, for the one that serves. This is not to say that individuals and families that do not serve in uniform do not understand, it is just a different life.

I have long felt that my dad had a lifelong love affair with an idea, and the idea is America. What we are, and what we can be as a country was central to his thoughts and desires. My dad was also a very "tough" guy. I'm referring to his emotional make up. I recall seeing or hearing my dad cry three times in my life. When his mother died, I saw him cry at her funeral. In 1976, we had a gathering at our house at Davis Monthan Air Force Base on the third anniversary of my dad's release from North Vietnam, a day we always referred to as "Freedom Day." My brother Steve gave my dad the button he had made in 1970 after we learned that my dad was a POW. The button reads "My Dad Is Alive." This brought tears to my dad's eyes.

Additionally, I remember a day in August of 2003. I was sitting at my desk in my home office in Tucson, Arizona, when my phone rang. I answered the phone, and it was my dad. This was the one and only time I heard my dad crying, almost uncontrollably. This was the day that Retired General Bill Creech died. My dad had worked for General Creech, and after they both retired, they talked often and became good friends. Through the tears my dad explained that America had lost a true patriot. This was also the day that I truly understood that there is a difference between being patriotic and being a patriot. I consider myself and my brothers to be very patriotic, an adjective that you might add to a description of the three of us. My dad however was a true patriot. In his case the word is a verb and describes a life of action, of doing, of caring, and of giving everything of himself to the "idea" that is America.

MEMORIES

While My Dad Was Gone and After His Return

The Day My Dad Was Shot Down

My dad was shot down on May 5th, 1967. I was just shy of my sixth birthday. We lived in a small apartment on Golf Links Road, in Tucson, Arizona. I do not remember the day that the Air Force came to our apartment to notify my mom; but, I recall my mom recounting the events of that day, many years later. I was likely at school when the Air Force arrived. I was attending Diez Elementary School and was finishing my kindergarten year.

My recollection is that a high-ranking Air Force officer, the base chaplain from Davis Monthan Air Force Base, and a nurse were all at the door when my mom answered the bell. The Air Force Officer asked if they could come in to talk with my mom. Her reply was simple and direct, "Dead or Alive?" My mom was very matter of fact and could not stand any anticipation or build up for what she knew was coming. They repeated their request to come inside, and she said "No, you are not coming in until you tell me, Dead or Alive?" At this point, they relayed the basics. "Your husband has been shot down in North Vietnam. He and his copilot both ejected, and two parachutes were seen descending to the ground."

I am unaware of the conversation that came after that one; but, this story has impacted my entire life. As the son of a lifelong Air Force fighter pilot, it is very challenging for me to hear about, read about, or watch the news or a movie, where they discuss the notification to the family. For example, when I watched the movie Saving Private Ryan, the single hardest scene for me to watch was when the mother is standing at the kitchen sink washing dishes, and she sees a car driving to her farm in the distance. She slowly makes her way to the front porch as the car draws nearer, and as they arrive in her front yard and exit the car, she collapses to the porch, knowing that the Army has arrived to tell a mother the worst news possible.

The National Football League Makes an Impact

I am not sure how old I was, but I was likely eight- or nine-years old. My mom received a questionnaire in the mail. My memory is that Johnny Unitas was involved in the project, but I could be wrong about that. At any rate, the questionnaire was sent to wives of POW/MIA husbands, and asked questions about their children. Given that I have two brothers and no sisters, I only remember the questions asked about the boys. Again, my recollection is fuzzy here, so the questionnaire could have been for both boys and girls with the same questions. The question for boys, was simply, "what is your favorite football team?" I was at an age where I was not aware of professional football. Clearly, the organizers of this initiative had given thought to this possibility and provided a sheet that had images of all the NFL football helmets.

My mom asked me about my favorite football team, and I simply responded, "I don't know." She showed me the page with all the helmet images, and I said, "I like the purple one with the horn on it." For Christmas that year, I received several presents directly from the Minnesota Viking organization. I received a mini football, a wall pennant, a poster for my wall, and a team photo taken at the old Metropolitan Stadium in Bloomington, Minnesota. My older brother received the same gifts from the Philadelphia Eagles and my younger brother from the Chicago Bears. That generosity locked me in as a lifelong Minnesota Vikings fan.

Flying on Air Force One (Number Two)

Let me start this story by sharing that I fully understand that Air Force One is technically only Air Force One when the

President is on the plane. This story is about the actual planes that are used to transport the President or Vice President and their families. During my dad's captivity, the Air Force allowed us to fly on military aircraft to travel.

It was a fantastic benefit for our family, given there were four of us, my mom, my two brothers and me. My mom was born and raised in Edinburgh, Scotland. This benefit allowed us to fly from Tucson, Arizona, to Edinburgh without purchasing commercial tickets. My mom was given an Air Force liaison, who would help with all the arrangements. The only thing that was required on our part, was a bit of flexibility. There was no schedule of flights for us to review and pick from, the way you do with commercial airlines. My mom would call her liaison and let him know when we wanted to fly, and where we were going.

The beginning and end of our flights might vary by a day or two depending on availability. We also would hopscotch our way to our destination. For example, we might fly from Tucson to Omaha, and then have to spend a night waiting for a flight from Omaha to Langley AFB, Virginia, and so on, to our destination. I remember on a return trip from Scotland, we were in Virginia, staying with friends, waiting for the Air Force to call, and let us know our next flight. They called to let us know we needed to come to Andrews AFB late in the day, early evening.

When we arrived, the plane that was waiting, was the Presidential plane. We were told it was Air Force One, number two, or the plane that transports the President when number one is being serviced. It was also the plane that transports the Vice President. I just know it was the thrill of a lifetime. We flew from Andrews AFB, Maryland, to Omaha on that plane, and our seats were in the Presidential suite at the rear of the plane. WOW, what an experience for a young child.

Defining My Relationship with My Dad – Six Little Words

I was five years old, and my dad was leaving for Thailand, a place I had never heard of. This would ultimately lead him to Vietnam. I stood at the gate that led out of our small apartment in

Tucson Arizona, held my arm in the air, made a fist, and he looked back at me and said, “See you in a little while, son.”

Six years later, my dad stepped off an airplane at March Air Force Base, California. I watched him come down the stairs and walk over to the four of us. When it was my turn to greet my dad, he knelt down, looked me in my eyes and said, “I’m sorry son, I told you I would see you in a little while, and it was a little longer than a little while, but I’m home.”

I was almost six years old when he left and twelve when he came home. I had no idea then that those six words: “see you in a little while,” would become a cornerstone of our relationship.

He told me repeatedly that he did not like the word “goodbye,” because he thought it sounded so “final.”

Throughout the years, no matter where he was, a far-off Air Force Base, at home in Columbia with Linda, at the College World Series watching his “Mighty Beavs” win it all or sitting with his brother and sister-in-law at the Steamboat Inn in Oregon, when we spoke, every single conversation ended with “see you in a little while,” never goodbye.

So, on the day that we honored and celebrated my dad’s life after his death, it was only fitting that I said, “see you in a little while, dad.”

My Dad Apologizes

This is one of the most impactful memories I have of my dad immediately following his release and return to Tucson. One afternoon, my dad gathered my brothers and me and took us out onto our back porch for a talk. I should step back and tell you that my dad graduated from Oregon State University. During his college days, he was a member of a fraternity. In the 1950s, it was very common to initiate new fraternity pledges with the use of a wooden paddle. The pledge would have to bend over and take “hits” with the paddle to the rear end. While it may sound kind of funny, being the recipient really does hurt. When I was very young, before my dad left for Thailand and Vietnam, if my older brother Steve and I got into trouble, my dad would get his wooden paddles from his fraternity days and use them to spank us. I do not think my younger brother ever received the spanking from the paddle, as he was only two years old when my dad left for Thailand.

So, there we are on the back porch with my dad, and he says to the three of us boys, "for the past six years, boys, people have been hitting and beating me whenever they felt like it, and there was nothing I could do to stop them. I'm sorry I ever hit you with those paddles. I will never touch you again."

It became very clear to me as I got older, the memory of paddling us boys created a huge burden on my dad's conscience. He had six long years to think about his actions, and he desperately wanted to correct it. He definitely did that. His actions also left an indelible mark on me as a parent. I have never disciplined my children using physical punishment.

Number One Responsibility of Leadership

Throughout my dad's life, he was always teaching, sharing, and working to develop leadership qualities in those who were around him. He did this in his professional life, as well as his personal life. It might be easy as his son, to think of this as "lecturing," and admittedly, sometimes it felt like that. However, one of those lessons that has always stuck with me that came directly from my dad: "…the number one responsibility of leadership, is to develop the next generation of leaders." He set an unbelievable example in this regard. Long after his retirement from the Air Force in 1984, he dedicated himself to imparting his lessons on those who followed him. Although he was an Air Force guy through and through, he was very involved with the Army Leadership at Fort Jackson in Columbia, SC. They regularly sought out my dad to speak to their officers and share lessons with them. He truly "lived" his belief in developing the next generation of leaders.

My Dad Speaking to the Leadership at Fort Jackson

A Visit to Hao Lo

Throughout my adult life I have often pondered a question: "If I had the opportunity to visit Hao Lo Prison in Hanoi, would I want to do so?" My answer was not an overwhelming, "Yes, I can't wait to do that." It was more of an answer of yes, but with a great deal of trepidation. I think I was always concerned about the emotion it would generate in me. Well, in the summer of 2019, we planned a family trip to Asia. We knew that we would visit Beijing, Shanghai, Hong Kong, and Singapore. When we discussed other locations to visit, I concluded that I could not go all that way to Asia, and not visit Hanoi. Given the significant impact this location had on my entire family. We added three days in Hanoi to our itinerary. My wife, my children and I all found Vietnam to be a wonderful country filled with wonderful people. The tours we experienced, the food we ate, and the people were all spectacular.

One of our tours included a visit to Hao Lo Prison. I would say this part of our trip was incredibly somber. My children are very aware of their grandfather's service and what this place represented. We had a wonderful tour guide for the day; however, he was not aware of our background and my dad's service. During our time at Hao Lo, he explained that his father had served in military intelligence during the war, and that although there may have been a few instances of bad treatment, this was perfectly normal, and that the treatment was expected to gain information. I chose not to engage the tour guide in conversation about this subject, namely because I was a visitor in his country, and secondly because I did not think it would be a productive conversation.

My son did, however, let the guide know at one point that his grandfather, my dad, had been held in North Vietnam for six years as a POW. This news seemed to deter further conversation about this subject.

The most difficult point in our tour, was looking into one of the actual cells that is part of the tour of Hao Lo. It made me very sad to have this glimpse into a very dark place where my dad spent so much time alone.

The "Doorknob" Story

I should start by saying that my two brothers and I have all been told this story, in some form, at some point in our lives. For me, it was many years ago. I was in my home office and having a bad day at work. I cannot remember what had made it a bad day. I know that sometime in the middle of the afternoon, my dad called me on my office phone. He was just calling to check in and see how I was doing. Given that he was catching me on a particularly bad day, when he asked how I was doing, I proceeded to tell him my story of woe about my bad day. Like the awesome father he was, he simply gave me the space I needed to explain my bad day to him. As my story ran out of steam, he asked if I was finished. I said yes, and then he took over.

He asked me to walk out of my office and over to the front door of my house. When I arrived at the front door and told him I was standing there, he asked me if there was a doorknob on the door. In a somewhat frustrated tone, I said, "It's a door Dad, of course there is a doorknob."

His reply to me was simple and direct. He said, “Son, any time there is a doorknob on the ‘inside,’ you’re having a good day.” My attitude about my bad day was instantly transformed, and the reality of living in freedom washed over me. After six years of living in captivity, his ability to provide much needed “perspective” was very fine tuned.

4th ALLIED P.O.W. WING
4
RETURN WITH HONOR

www.ingramcontent.com/pod-product-compliance
Lightning Source LLC
LaVergne TN
LVHW011656100826
845155LV00004B/14

* 9 7 9 8 9 8 9 5 6 2 0 0 8 *